PREFACE

1. Scope

This publication provides doctrine for the command and control of joint land operations by a joint force land component commander (JFLCC). It addresses considerations for forming and establishing a functional land force component with a designated JFLCC and for planning, executing, and assessing joint force land operations across the range of military operations.

2. Purpose

This publication has been prepared under the direction of the Chairman of the Joint Chiefs of Staff (CJCS). It sets forth joint doctrine to govern the activities and performance of the Armed Forces of the United States in joint operations and provides the doctrinal basis for interagency coordination and for US military involvement in multinational operations. It provides military guidance for the exercise of authority by combatant commanders and other joint force commanders (JFCs) and prescribes joint doctrine for operations, education, and training. It provides military guidance for use by the Armed Forces in preparing their appropriate plans. It is not the intent of this publication to restrict the authority of the JFC from organizing the force and executing the mission in a manner the JFC deems most appropriate to ensure unity of effort in the accomplishment of the overall objective.

3. Application

a. Joint doctrine established in this publication applies to the joint staff, commanders of combatant commands, subunified commands, joint task forces, subordinate components of these commands, the Services, and combat support agencies.

b. The guidance in this publication is authoritative; as such, this doctrine will be followed except when, in the judgment of the commander, exceptional circumstances dictate otherwise. If conflicts arise between the contents of this publication and the contents of Service publications, this publication will take precedence unless the CJCS, normally in coordination with the other members of the Joint Chiefs of Staff, has provided more current and specific guidance. Commanders of forces operating as part of a multinational (alliance or coalition) military command should follow multinational doctrine and procedures ratified by the United States. For doctrine and procedures not ratified by the United States, commanders should evaluate and follow the multinational command's doctrine and procedures, and where applicable and consistent with US law, regulations, and doctrine.

For the Chairman of the Joint Chiefs of Staff:

DAVID L. GOLDFEIN, Lt Gen, USAF
Director, Joint Staff

Intentionally Blank

SUMMARY OF CHANGES
REVISION OF JOINT PUBLICATION 3-31
DATED 29 JUNE 2010

- **Establishes Department of Defense definition of land domain.**

- **Expands discussion of land-centric joint task force advantages, disadvantages, and impacts.**

- **Clarifies joint force land component commander's authority and responsibilities in theater joint operation area.**

- **Adds section on cyberspace operations.**

- **Explains the information operations cell and cyberspace support elements activities in relation to the joint force land component command.**

- **Discusses how to integrate joint force land component command communication systems.**

- **Clarifies the function of joint network operations communications within a joint force land component command.**

- **Expands discussion of operational approach and design in relation joint land operations.**

- **Deletes discussion of traditional warfare and irregular warfare to eliminate redundancy with other joint publications.**

- **Reduces material on stability operations.**

- **Provides more material on mitigation of civilian casualties.**

- **Adds information on countering weapons of mass destruction.**

- **Expands discussion of defense support of civil authorities.**

- **Replaces single-Service theory and terminology with approved joint positions.**

- **Updates figures, quotes, and vignettes.**

Intentionally Blank

TABLE OF CONTENTS

Intentionally Blank

EXECUTIVE SUMMARY
COMMANDER'S OVERVIEW

- **Provides an Introduction to Joint Land Operations**

- **Explains How to Establish a Joint Force Land Component and Its Command and Control Structure**

- **Explains Planning and Assessment of Joint Land Operations**

- **Presents the Forms of Joint Land Operations and Their Relation to Joint Functions and Other Operations and Capabilities**

Introduction

Joint Land Operations

The land domain is the area of the Earth's surface ending at the high water mark and overlapping with the maritime domain in the landward segment of the littorals.

Joint land operations include any type of joint military operations, singly or in combination, performed across the range of military operations with joint land forces (Army, Marine, or special operations) made available by Service components in support of the joint force commander's (JFC's) operation or campaign objectives, or in support of other components of the joint force.

Joint land operations include **land control operations.** Such operations are conducted to establish local military superiority in land operational areas.

Organizing the Joint Land Force

If the JFC does not choose to retain control at the JFC level, there are four primary options available to the JFC for employing land forces from two or more components:

- Subordinate unified command for land operations (available only to a combatant commander).

- Subordinate joint task forces.

- Service components.

- Functional land component with joint force land component commander (JFLCC).

The Joint Force Land Component Command

Designated Authorities

The JFC defines the authority and responsibilities of the functional component commanders based upon the concept of operations (CONOPS), and may alter this

---

authority during the course of an operation. The designation of a JFLCC normally occurs when forces of significant size and capability of more than one Service component participate in a land operation and the JFC determines that doing this will achieve unity of command and effort among land forces.

Roles and Responsibilities

The responsibilities of the JFLCC include, but are not limited to, the following:

- Advising the JFC on the proper employment of forces made available for tasking.

- Developing the joint land operation plan (OPLAN)/operation order (OPORD) in support of the JFC's CONOPS and optimizing the operations of task-organized land forces.

- Directing the execution of land operations as specified by the JFC.

- Coordinating the planning and execution of joint land operations with the other components and supporting agencies.

Designating an Area of Operations

Areas of operations (AOs) are defined by the JFC for surface (land and maritime) forces.

The JFLCC establishes an operational framework for the AO that assigns responsibilities to subordinate land commanders and maximizes the operational capabilities of all subordinate elements.

The JFLCC is the supported commander within the land AO designated by the JFC. Within the designated AO, the JFLCC has the authority to designate target priority, effects, and timing of fires in order to integrate and synchronize maneuver, fires, and interdiction.

Organizing

The JFC establishing a functional component command has the authority to designate its commander. Normally, the Service component commander with the preponderance of forces to be tasked and the ability to command and control (C2) those forces will be designated as the functional component commander;

however, the JFC will always consider the mission, nature, and duration of the operation, force capabilities, and the C2 capabilities in selecting a commander.

As the JFC develops the CONOPS, the Service and functional components develop their supporting plans. The JFC, working with the functional and Service components, sources the actual forces needed by the JFLCC. Based upon JFC guidance, Service components designate specific units to report to the JFC, which are assigned a command relationship with the JFLCC.

Forming the Staff and Command Element

The JFLCC's staff is organized based upon the mission and forces assigned and attached.

The most likely candidates for a JFLCC are Army corps or a Marine air-ground task force (most likely a Marine expeditionary force). For smaller scale operations, a contingency command post from an Army Service component command, an Army division, or a Marine expeditionary brigade could be employed. Ideally, the JFLCC and the deputy JFLCC or chief of staff would come from different Services. This construct should be replicated throughout the staff leadership to ensure an understanding of the distinct capabilities of each Service to optimize employment of the forces.

Command Relationships

The JFC establishes the command relationships and assignment of forces to accomplish mission objectives. The JFC will also specify the command relationships between the functional components and Service components.

The JFLCC reports directly to the JFC and advises the JFC on the proper employment of land forces assigned, attached, or made available. The JFC has the authority to assign missions, redirect efforts, and direct coordination among subordinate commanders. The JFC may also establish support relationships among components.

The JFLCC will normally be a Service component commander. As Service component commander, the JFLCC normally exercises operational control over its respective Service forces. As a functional component commander, the JFLCC normally exercises tactical control over other forces or capabilities made available for tasking, or receives support as determined by the JFC.

Planning and Assessment

Support to Joint Operation Planning

The JFLCC's planners must first frame the strategic and operational problem by developing an understanding of the situation before addressing operational design and ultimately OPLANs. Several cognitive models exist to assist JFLCC's and their staffs as they plan and execute joint land operations. The operational approach is the commander's visualization of how the operations should transform current conditions at end state.

Operational Planning Considerations

The primary difference between planning for single-Service employment and joint land operations is synchronizing the unique capabilities and limitations of each force to achieve unity of effort. This requires an understanding of these capabilities and limitations across all staff functions, but it is particularly important in the joint planning group (JPG). The JPG must have knowledgeable members from each Service in all functional areas. With these key personnel and appropriate liaison officers from the major subordinate commands in place, the planning process provides sufficient consideration of the capabilities of each Service.

Joint Land Operations Plan

JFLCC joint land OPLANs, joint land operation plans in concept format, and OPORDs convey how the land force helps achieve the JFC's mission. The plans developed by the JFLCC describe the intended conduct of joint land operations that support the attainment of JFC's objectives.

Assessment

Commanders and their staffs determine relevant assessment actions and measures during planning. They consider assessment measures as early as mission analysis and include assessment measures and related guidance in commander and staff estimates.

Normally, the JFLCC's chief of staff, assisted by the operations directorate of a joint staff and the intelligence directorate of a joint staff, is responsible for coordinating assessment activities. The chief of staff is normally also assisted by an assessment special staff section which may include personnel to do operations research and systems analysis, sociocultural experts, and others. For subordinate commanders' staffs, this may be accomplished by equivalent elements within Service components.

Assessment occurs at all levels of military operations. Even in operations that do not include combat, assessment of progress is just as important and can be more complex than traditional combat assessment. As a general rule, the level at which a specific operation, task, or action is directed should be the level at which such activity is assessed.

Operations

Forms of Operations

Major operations and campaigns, whether or not they involve large-scale ground combat, normally will include some level of both offense and defense.

Offensive land operations are combat operations conducted to defeat and destroy enemy land forces and seize terrain, resources, and population centers. Offensive land operations impose the commander's will on the enemy.

Defensive operations are combat operations conducted to defeat an enemy attack, gain time, economize forces, and develop conditions favorable for offensive or stability operations. Defensive land control operations retain terrain, guard populations, and protect critical capabilities against enemy attacks and are used to gain time and economize forces so offensive tasks can be executed elsewhere.

Stability operations encompass various military missions, tasks, and activities conducted outside the US in coordination with other instruments of national power to maintain or reestablish a safe and secure environment, provide essential governmental services, emergency infrastructure reconstruction, and humanitarian relief. Stability operations will not only include stability tasks, but will often have elements of offense and defense.

Defense Support of Civil Authorities

Military operations inside the US and its territories, though limited in many respects, are conducted to accomplish two missions: homeland defense and defense support of civil authorities (DSCA). A JFLCC is often used to provide C2 for land operations for DSCA. DSCA consists of Department of Defense support to US civil authorities for domestic emergencies, both man-made and natural, and for designated law enforcement and other activities, such as national special security events.

Joint Functions

Functions that are common to joint operations at all levels of war fall into six basic groups—C2, intelligence, fires, movement and maneuver, protection, and sustainment.

The JFLCC can choose from a wide variety of joint and Service capabilities and combine them in various ways to perform joint functions and accomplish the mission. The joint land OPLAN/OPORD describes the way joint land forces and assets are used together to perform joint functions and tasks. However, forces and assets are not characterized by the functions for which the JFLCC is employing them. A single force or asset can perform multiple functions simultaneously or sequentially while executing a single task.

The JFLCC and staff must also monitor and may coordinate and synchronize the support functions (e.g., logistics, personnel support) that impact joint land operations.

CONCLUSION

This publication provides doctrine for the C2 of joint land operations by a JFLCC. It addresses considerations for forming and establishing a functional land force component with a designated JFLCC and for planning, executing, and assessing joint force land operations across the range of military operations.

CHAPTER I
INTRODUCTION

"Modern land warfare is the most conclusive, yet the least exclusive, of the geographically focused branches of conflict. Because the belligerents in modern strategic history, with only minor and partial exceptions, have been territorially defined, victory or defeat on land has been all but equivalent to victory or defeat in war."

Colin S. Gray, *Modern Strategy*, 1999

1. Background

a. **Command and control (C2) of joint land operations is fundamental to warfare. Having a land component commander (LCC) is not new to the Armed Forces of the United States.** The Allies in World War II successfully employed separate joint or multinational LCC headquarters in several theaters. These land component commands ensured proper coordination with other components and freed the multinational force commander to focus on overall strategy. After the Allied repulses at the battle of the Kasserine Pass in 1943 due to poor **command relationships,** General Dwight D. Eisenhower restructured his Allied Forces in North Africa. Not only were all air elements brought under centralized control, but all land forces were also consolidated under General Sir Harold Alexander's 18th Army Group. This structure was the first modern **combined** organization with coequal land, sea, and air component commanders under separate commanders and contributed significantly to the defeat of the Axis in North Africa by May 1943. For the Normandy invasion in June 1944, Eisenhower again subordinated US Army forces (ARFOR) under a multinational LCC, British Field Marshal Bernard Law Montgomery.

b. During World War II in the Pacific, US Army and United States Marine Corps (USMC) land forces habitually operated together. Lieutenant General Holland M. Smith, USMC, commanded both US Army and USMC forces in the Mariana Islands campaign. Perhaps the most notable instance of Army and Marine Corps **integration** occurred during the battle for Okinawa in 1945. Lieutenant General Simon Bolivar Buckner, US Army (Commanding General Tenth Army and Task Force 56), commanded the joint expeditionary force with the mission of seizing Okinawa as a shaping operation for the eventual invasion of the Japanese home islands. Tenth Army consisted of XXIV Army Corps, III Amphibious Corps, and a Tactical Air Force that consisted of the 2d Marine Aircraft Wing and Army Air Force elements under Major General F.P. Mulcahy, USMC. The Island Command under Army Major General F.G. Wallace provided Army-level enabling troops that also had the primary mission of establishing the base complexes for subsequent operations. Joint land operations at Okinawa should have provided the model for a joint force land component command.

c. Following World War II, joint land operations became the exception as the lessons of World War II were lost. Frequently, officers serving as theater commanders attempted with varying degrees of success to also serve as multinational or joint LCCs. Campaigns such as in Korea in 1950 and Vietnam during 1965-1972 were fought without unifying land

British General Sir Harold Alexander, Lieutenant General George S. Patton, and Rear Admiral Alan G. Kirk inspect invasion task force for Operation HUSKY off the coast of Sicily. Alexander was to become the land component commander of the allied forces in March 1943. (Official US Navy photograph)

operations under a single component commander or headquarters for C2. In March 1999 neither a combined nor a joint forces land component command was established for either the North Atlantic Treaty Organization (NATO) Operation ALLIED FORCE or its associated US operation.

d. Operation ENDURING FREEDOM (OEF) and Operation IRAQI FREEDOM (OIF) (Afghanistan and Iraq). In June 1998, General Anthony Zinni, Commander of United States Central Command (USCENTCOM), designated Lieutenant General Tommy Franks, Commander of US Army Central Command (ARCENT) and Third US Army, as his joint force land component commander (JFLCC) for any operations that might occur in the Middle East. Subsequently, when Lieutenant General Franks became the commander of USCENTCOM, he similarly designated his replacement as the JFLCC in the war plans as well. Consequently, after the terrorist attacks of 11 September 2001, Lieutenant General P.T. Mikolashek assumed control of the land operations in the Afghanistan joint operations area (JOA) in November 2001 for the conduct of OEF and was designated the coalition forces land component commander (CFLCC). As such, Lieutenant General Mikolashek

WORLD WAR II JOINT COMMAND

"General [Sir Harold R.L.G.] Alexander was to become the deputy commander of the Allied force. Admiral [Sir Andrew Browne] Cunningham was to remain as my naval [chief]. And Air Chief Marshall Sir Arthur W. Tedder was assigned as the [chief] of the air forces. ... This development was extraordinarily pleasing to me because it meant, first and foremost, complete unity of action in the central Mediterranean and it provided for needed machinery for effective tactical and strategic co-ordination. ... [after the Kasserine battle] the ground command on the Tunisian front was placed under General Alexander. The latter...was able to devote his entire attention to daily tactical co-ordination.

General of the Army Dwight D. Eisenhower, *Crusade in Europe,* 1948

controlled a unique combination of Army, Marine Corps, special forces, and Northern Alliance allies during the defeat of the Taliban and their Al-Qaeda allies.

e. In September 2002, Lieutenant General David McKiernan replaced Lieutenant General Mikolashek as the CFLCC. From September through March 2003, he supervised the establishment and preparation of CFLCC theater forces, coordinated with the other components and coalition partners, received in Kuwait almost 300,000 troops, and completed the coalition land operations plan. The ARCENT Headquarters was modified to include more than 70 Marines and a total of over 150 joint and coalition officers. Beginning 20 March 2003, he conducted OIF supervising two large corps-sized forces (V Corps and I Marine Expeditionary Force [MEF]) as well as more than 56,000 theater-level troops during the defeat of Iraqi forces. With the fall of Saddam Hussein's regime in May, Lieutenant General McKiernan assumed duties as the Commander of Coalition Joint Task Force Iraq, initially responsible for conducting stabilization and reconstruction operations countrywide. From 15 June 2003 to the present, ARCENT has operated from Kuwait where it serves as the theater CFLCC responsible for coordinating land planning and for ensuring uninterrupted logistic support for simultaneous operations in Afghanistan, Iraq, and elsewhere in the USCENTCOM area of responsibility (AOR). Between 2004 and 2010, Multinational Corps-Iraq served as the de facto CFLCC for Multinational Force—Iraq and directly supervised most of the Army, Marine Corps, and coalition land forces conducting stability, reconstruction, and counterinsurgency (COIN) operations in Iraq. Similarly, the International Security and Assistance Force Joint Command has served as the de facto CFLCC in Afghanistan since 2009.

2. Joint Land Operations

a. In the 20th century, joint and **multinational operations** have encompassed the full diversity of air, land, maritime, and space forces operating throughout the operational area. Advances in capabilities among all forces and the ability to communicate over great distances have made the application of military power in the 21st century more dependent on the ability of commanders to synchronize and integrate **joint land operations** with other components' operations. Many of these advances have been realized through the use of cyberspace and the electromagnetic spectrum (EMS), which has enabled the US military and allies to communicate and reach across geographic and geopolitical boundaries. However, these advances have also led to increased vulnerabilities and a critical dependence on cyberspace and the EMS for the US and its allies.

b. Joint land operations include any type of joint military operations, singly or in combination, performed across the range of military operations with joint land forces (Army, Marine, or special operations) made available by Service components in support of the joint force commander's (JFC's) operation or campaign objectives, or in support of other components of the joint force. Joint land operations require synchronization and integration of all instruments of national power to achieve strategic and operational objectives. Normally, joint land operations will also involve multinational **land forces.**

c. Joint land operations includes **land control operations.** These are described as the employment of land forces, supported by maritime and air forces (as appropriate) to control vital land areas. Such operations are conducted to establish local military superiority in land **operational areas.** Land control operations may also be required to isolate, seize, or secure weapons of mass destruction (WMD) to prevent use, proliferation, or loss.

d. Joint Publication (JP) 3-0, *Joint Operations,* establishes the JFC's operational environment as composed of the air, land, maritime, and space domains as well as the information environment (which includes cyberspace). Domains are useful constructs to aid in visualizing and characterizing the physical environment in which operations are conducted. Nothing in the definitions of, or the use of the term domain, implies or mandates exclusivity, primacy, or C2 of that domain. C2 is established by the JFC based upon the most effective use of available resources to accomplish assigned missions. The **land domain** is the land area of the Earth's surface ending at the high water mark and overlapping with the maritime domain in the landward segment of the littorals. The land domain shares the Earth's surface with the maritime domain.

e. **Land operations** are conducted within a complex operational environment. Numbers of civilians, amount of valuable infrastructure, avenues of approach, freedom of vehicular movement, and communications functionality vary considerably among land environments, creating challenges for the JFLCC. In addition, urban or emerging subterranean environments require special consideration for the conduct of joint land operations. As a result, **joint land operations require an effective and efficient C2 structure to achieve success.**

See JP 3-06, Joint Urban Operations, *for capabilities and tasks that are unique to, or significantly challenged by, joint urban operations at the operational level.*

f. It is important to understand that in today's complex operational environment, adversary actions can be delivered on, from, within, and outside of the operational area, all with potentially global impacts and influence. To negate those threats, commanders at all levels should consider how space, cyberspace, and EMS capabilities enhance the effectiveness and execution of joint land operations. Furthermore, joint staffs should seek out experts who and capabilities that can enhance the effectiveness of land operations.

3. Organizing the Joint Land Force

a. The manner in which geographic combatant commanders (GCCs) organize their forces directly affects the C2, responsiveness, and versatility of joint force operations. Combatant commanders (CCDRs) **organize assigned and attached forces to accomplish the mission based on the CCDR's vision and concept of operations (CONOPS) as well as considerations of mission, enemy, terrain and weather, troops and support available, and time available.** Unity of action, centralized planning and direction, and **decentralized execution** are also key considerations. CCDRs can conduct operations through **subordinate unified commands,** subordinate joint task forces (JTFs), single-Service task forces (TFs), Service components, functional components, or a combination of Service and functional components.

b. Although not recommended due to the need to concentrate on JFC-level considerations, the JFC may elect to retain control of joint land operations within the joint force headquarters and directly integrate these with other operations. In making this decision, the JFC should consider the impact dual-hatting has on the staff as it is forced to simultaneously operate at strategic and operational levels. In those instances, the JFC would retain **command authority** and responsibility for all land forces and use the JFC staff with augmentation, as appropriate, to assist in planning and coordinating joint land operations. **If the JFC does not choose to retain control at the JFC level, there are four primary options available to the JFC for employing land forces from two or more components:**

(1) Subordinate **unified command** for land operations (available only to a CCDR).

(2) Subordinate JTF(s).

(3) Service components.

(4) Functional land component with **JFLCC.**

c. Each option has advantages and disadvantages the JFC and staff must consider prior to a decision to organize under a particular option. The following advantages and disadvantages are not all-inclusive but highlight some important issues that should be considered.

(1) **Subordinate Unified Command**

(a) Advantages: enduring unity of **command** and effort, **joint staff,** and the authority of a JFC including the authority to organize subordinate JTF and/or functional components.

(b) Disadvantages: separate subunified command commander/staff required and lead-time required to establish headquarters before execution.

(2) **Subordinate JTF**

PERSIAN GULF WAR EXAMPLE OF JOINT FORCE COMMANDER RETAINING CONTROL OF LAND FORCES

The Saudis had insisted on commanding all Arab forces. Yet the need to maintain unity of command called for establishing a land component commander in charge of all ground forces.... Political sensitivities argued against placing Arab forces under an American land commander. Technically, USCENTCOM [United States Central Command] did not control Arab-Islamic forces, and [General] Khalid was [General Norman A.] Schwarzkopf's political equal....

Schwarzkopf made the tough decision to retain the land component commander responsibility for himself, with [Lieutenant General Calvin A. H.] Waller [the USCENTCOM deputy commander] serving as his primary assistant for ground combat issues. The decision created numerous challenges and difficulties. Though [Lieutenant General John J.] Yeosock [the Third Army commander] was clearly charged with commanding the two US corps, Schwarzkopf was within his rights as the LCC [land component commander] in going directly to the corps commanders with instructions. From the other direction, the two US corps commanders dealt directly with Lieutenant General John J. Yeosock. Lieutenant General Charles Horner, as the joint force air component commander, could go directly to [Schwarzkopf], whereas Lieutenant General John J. Yeosock competed with the Arab command and the Marines [I MEF] [Marine Expeditionary Force] for Schwarzkopf's attention. This rather convoluted arrangement certainly went against the principles of simplicity and unity of command. That it was made to work as smoothly as it did was attributable to the powerful personalities and professionalism of the senior commanders.

SOURCE: Brigadier General Robert H. Scales Jr., *Certain Victory: The US Army in the Gulf War*

(a) Advantages: unity of command and effort, a joint staff, and the authority of a JFC, including the authority to organize subordinate functional components.

(b) Disadvantages: size of staff and lead time required to establish the headquarters before execution.

For a more detailed discussion of JTFs, see JP 3-33, Joint Task Force Headquarters.

(3) **Service Components**

(a) Advantages: simplified C2, requires no change in structure, JFC directly integrates **land operations** with other operations, and easier to establish prior to execution.

(b) Disadvantages: staff not integrated, liaison only; potential for ineffective use of assigned forces due to tasking and mission redundancies; JFC retains focus on the land battle; potential for JFC to lose focus on the operational interface; and no single focus for land forces, joint land operations, or coordination with other functional components.

---

(4) **Functional Land Component**

(a) Advantages: unity of effort, integrated staff, single voice for land forces and land operations (consolidated picture of land force capabilities/requirements to the JFC, staff, boards, and other functional components), single concept and focus of effort for land operations (an aspect of the plan rather than a function of coordination either horizontally or vertically), synchronized and integrated land force planning and execution (prioritization and therefore deconfliction of competing land force requirements).

(b) Disadvantages: JFLCC normally retains Service component responsibilities to the JFC (requires split focus of the staff), challenge of integrating staffs, more lead-time required to establish headquarters before execution, and sourcing the staffs.

d. No matter which option is selected, the JFC must designate responsibility for the conduct of joint land operations. Hereafter, the JFLCC will be used in this publication to discuss the responsibilities and functions of the commander designated to conduct joint land operations.

4. Forming Considerations

a. Not only can the **GCC** designate a JFLCC, but each subordinate JFC may also designate their own JFLCC. Consequently, there may be multiple LCCs, each with an organization, duties, and responsibilities tailored to the requirements of their specific JFC, within a single AOR. Where multiple **JOAs** each have **land operations** being conducted, the JFLCC designated directly by the GCC may also be designated the theater JFLCC. The primary responsibilities of the theater JFLCC may be to provide coordination with other theater-level functional components, to provide general support to the multiple JFLCCs within the AOR, to conduct theater-level planning, or to conduct joint reception, staging, onward movement, and integration (JRSOI) for the entire joint land force. The most likely candidate for a theater JFLCC is the Army Service component command (ASCC)/theater army. Within a JOA or when there is only one JFLCC in an AOR, the JFC forms a functional land component to improve combat efficiency, unity of effort, weapons system management, component interaction, or control the land scheme of maneuver. **Forming a functional land component is a key organizational decision, which will significantly influence the conduct of land operations.** The following are some of the factors to be considered by the JFC in making such a decision. See Figure I-1.

b. **Mission. The mission requires that the capabilities and functions of more than one Service be directed toward closely related land objectives where unity of effort is a**

> *"We can make a land component command arrangement work. There will be no more occasions in the Central Command's area of operations where Marines will fight one ground war and the Army fights a different ground war. There will be one ground war and a single land component commander."*
>
> **General Anthony C. Zinni**
> **Commander, United States Central Command**
> **(August 1997-September 2000)**

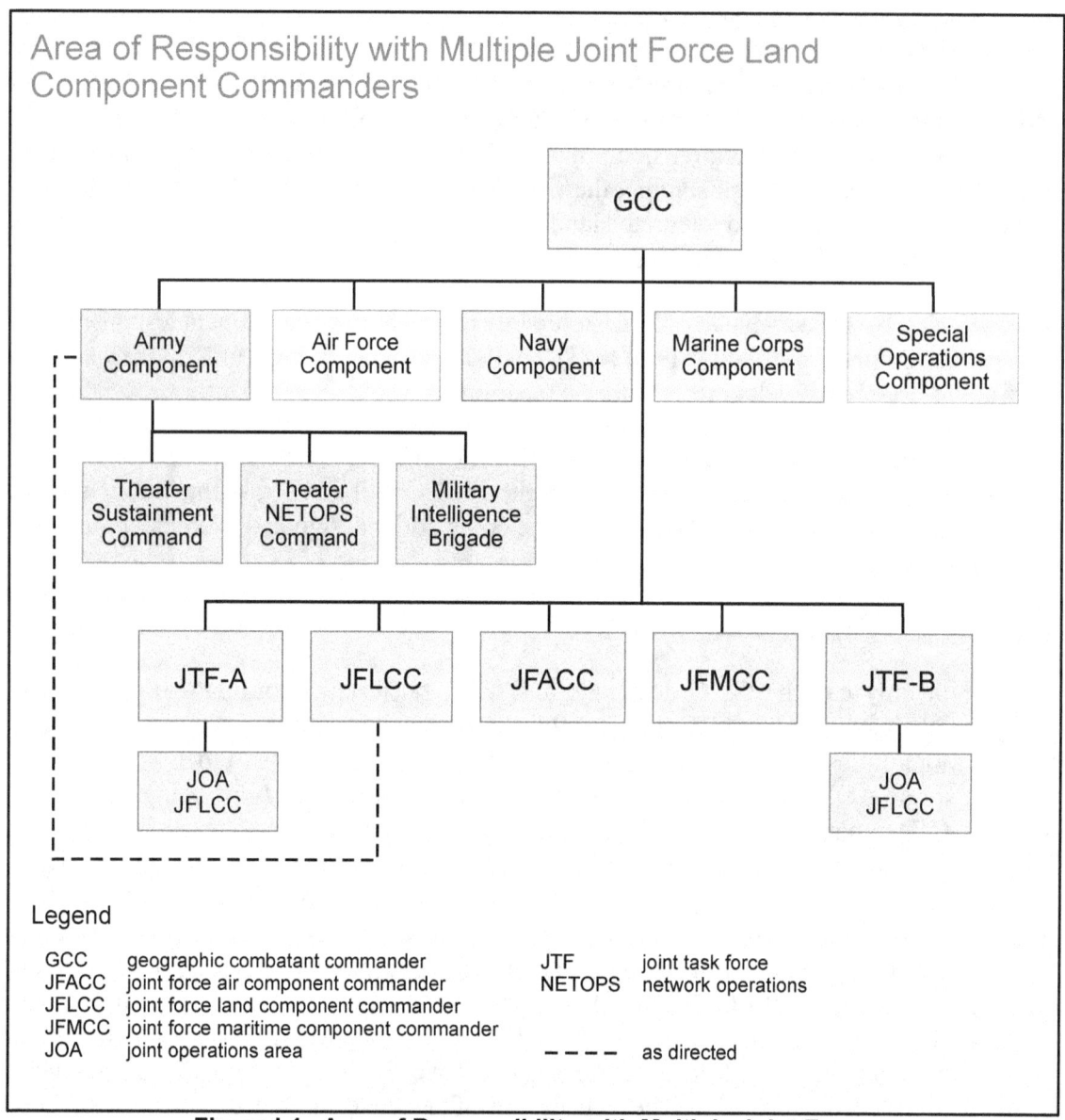

Figure I-1. Area of Responsibility with Multiple Joint Force Land Component Commanders

primary concern. Land forces are competing for limited joint force assets. The JFLCC contributes to the combat efficiency, prioritization and control of joint force assets, scheme of maneuver, and joint fires, as the situation requires. The JFLCC provides direction and control of land operations.

c. **Scope of Operations**

(1) When the scope of joint land operations is large in force size and/or operational area, the JFC needs to apportion responsibility among major operations or phases of operations and synchronize those operations. It may be advantageous, therefore, to establish functionally oriented commanders responsible for the major operations. **A functional land**

component may be designated any time the forces of two or more Military Departments operate in the same operational area.

(2) The unity of command offered by a JFLCC may be especially beneficial in geographically concentrated land operations as it provides singular focus, expedited decision making, and centralized coordination.

(a) **Level of Operations.** Regardless of size, when the scope of the operation requires an operational level command to directly link **land operations** to **campaign** or strategic objectives, a JFLCC can provide the linkage.

(b) **Span of Control.** The multiple complex tasks confronting the JFC may challenge the JFC's span of control and ability to oversee and influence each task. In addition, the **commander of a unified command should not act concurrently as the commander of a subordinate command,** such as a functional component command, without the prior approval of the Secretary of Defense (SecDef). Having a separate JFLCC allows resolution of joint issues at the functional component level and enhances component interaction at that level. The JFC has other responsibilities in the operational area that may require greater focus. If the operation can be controlled by one corps-sized unit, either an **Army corps** commander or a MEF commander could be designated as a JFLCC. If the mission requires more than one corps-sized unit, the preferred option is for the commander of either a field army or the **theater army** headquarters to be designated the JFLCC.

d. **Planning.** The formation of a functional land component with a JFLCC integrates planning beneath the level of the JFC for land operations. In addition, the designation of a JFLCC enhances the integration and synchronization of operational maneuver with fires by making the JFLCC the supported commander within their designated area of operations (AO).

e. **Duration.** Duration of operations must be long enough to warrant establishing a JFLCC. The duration of operations must be worth the costs in terms of time, personnel and staff training, C2, communications systems, intelligence architectures, and impact on flexibility. The decision to constitute a JFLCC should be made early enough in the JFC's planning cycle to facilitate establishment and preparation of the headquarters for **land operations** and allow time for generation of a comprehensive plan for the application of land power in support of the JFC. In the case of the US homeland, and the joint operations of homeland defense (HD) and defense support of civil authorities (DSCA), the formation of a joint force land component command has become a durable requirement as enduring threats to the homeland are both natural and man-made.

f. **Experience.** Designating a JFLCC, with an experienced land oriented staff, enhances the detailed planning, coordination, and execution of **joint land operations.**

g. **Multinational Operations.** Multinational operations are operations conducted by forces of two or more nations, usually undertaken within the structure of a coalition or alliance. Designating a multinational LCC provides for unity of effort for **land operations.** See Chapter III, "Planning and Assessment," for more on multinational operations.

For a more detailed discussion of multinational operations, see JP 3-16, Multinational Operations, *and Allied Joint Publication (AJP) 3.2,* Allied Joint Doctrine for Land Operations.

CHAPTER II
THE JOINT FORCE LAND COMPONENT COMMAND

"We can never forget that organization, no less than a bayonet or an aircraft carrier, is a weapon of war. We owe it to our Soldiers, our Sailors, our Airmen, and our Marines to ensure that this weapon is lean enough, flexible enough, and tough enough to help them win, if God forbid, that ever becomes necessary."

Congressman Bill Nichols, Hearings for the Goldwater-Nichols Act, 1986

SECTION A. ESTABLISHING THE JOINT FORCE LAND COMPONENT COMMAND

1. Designated Authorities

a. The JFC has the authority to organize forces to best accomplish the assigned mission based on the **CONOPS.**   The JFC establishes **subordinate commands**, assigns responsibilities, establishes or delegates appropriate command relationships, and establishes coordinating instructions for the component commanders. Sound organization provides for unity of command, centralized planning and direction, and decentralized execution. Unity of command is necessary for effectiveness and efficiency. Centralized planning and direction is essential for controlling and coordinating the efforts of the forces. Decentralized execution is essential because no one commander can control the detailed actions of a large number of units or individuals. When organizing joint forces, simplicity and clarity are critical; **by making the JFLCC the single commander for joint land operations, the JFC has the ability to enhance synchronization of operations not only between US ground and component forces, but also with multinational land forces.**

See JP 1, Doctrine for the Armed Forces of the United States, *for additional doctrinal guidance on establishing the land component command and designating the JFLCC.*

b. **The JFC defines the authority and responsibilities of the functional component commanders** based upon the CONOPS, and may alter this authority during the course of an operation.

c. The designation of a JFLCC normally occurs when forces of significant size and capability of more than one Service component participate in a land operation and the JFC determines that doing this will achieve unity of command and effort among land forces.

2. Roles and Responsibilities

The JFLCC's overall responsibilities and roles are to plan, coordinate, and employ forces made available for tasking in support of the JFC's CONOPS. **The responsibilities of the JFLCC include, but are not limited to, the following:**

a. Advising the JFC on the proper employment of forces made available for tasking. Developing, integrating, maintaining, and sharing with the JFC an accurate representation of the land common operational picture (COP) (objects and events) within the JFLCC's operational area, as an input to the JFC's COP.

b. Developing the joint land operation plan (OPLAN)/operation order (OPORD) in support of the JFC's CONOPS and optimizing the operations of task-organized land forces. (See Appendix C, "Joint Land Operation Plan and Order Development.") The JFLCC issues planning guidance to all subordinate and supporting elements and analyzes proposed courses of action (COAs). The intent is to concentrate combat power at critical times and places to accomplish strategic, operational, and tactical objectives.

c. Directing the execution of land operations as specified by the JFC, which includes making timely adjustments to the tasking of forces and capabilities made available. The JFLCC coordinates changes with affected component commanders as appropriate.

d. Coordinating the planning and execution of joint land operations with the other components and supporting agencies.

e. Evaluating the results of land operations to include the effectiveness of interdiction operations and forwarding these results to the JFC to support the **combat assessment** effort.

f. Synchronizing and integrating movement and maneuver, fires, and interdiction in support of land operations.

g. Designating the target priorities, effects, and timing for joint land operations.

h. Planning and conducting personnel recovery (PR) in support of joint land operations and for isolating events occurring within assigned operational area or as tasked by the JFC. Performing duties of the joint force supported commander for PR, if designated.

See JP 3-50, Personnel Recovery, *for additional guidance on PR.*

i. Providing mutual support to other components by conducting operations such as suppression of enemy air defenses and suppression of threats to maritime operations.

j. Coordinating with other functional and Service components' sustainment support in accomplishment of JFC objectives.

k. Providing an assistant or deputy to the **area air defense commander (AADC)** for land-based joint theater integrated air and missile defense (AMD) operations and coordination as determined by the JFC.

l. Supporting the JFCs **information operations** (IO) by developing the IO requirements that support land operations and synchronizing the land force information-related capabilities (IRCs) when directed.

m. Establishing standard operating procedures (SOPs) and other directives based on JFC guidance.

n. Providing inputs into the JFC-approved joint operational area air defense plan (AADP) and the airspace control plan (ACP).

o. Planning and determining requirements for, and coordinating implementation of, the JFLCC's communications systems, integrating them into the theater's Department of Defense information networks (DODIN) architecture.

p. Integrating cyberspace operations (CO) into plans. Offensive cyberspace operations will typically be conducted in direct support of the JFC. The JFLCC conducts defensive cyberspace operations (DCO) and DODIN operations throughout all phases of the operation.

For more information on joint C2 planning and utilization of networked capabilities, refer to the Chairman of the Joint Chiefs of Staff Instruction (CJCSI) 3155.01, Global Command and Control System–Joint (GCCS-J), Operational Framework Policy, *and CJCSI 3151.01,* Global Command and Control System Common Operational Picture Reporting Requirements.

q. Integrating special operations, as required, into overall land operations.

For additional information on special operations forces (SOF), refer to JP 3-05, Special Operations.

r. Performing joint security functions, such as serving as the **joint security coordinator (JSC),** as designated by the JFC.

See JP 3-10, Joint Security Operations in Theater, *for additional guidance on joint security functions.*

s. Supervising detainee operations as designated by the JFC.

See JP 3-63, Detainee Operations, *for additional guidance on detainee operations.*

t. Facilitating interorganizational coordination, as required.

See JP 3-08, Interorganizational Coordination During Joint Operations, *for additional guidance on interorganizational coordination.*

u. **Performing the duties of the space coordinating authority (SCA),** if designated. The individual designated to be the JFLCC may also be designated to be the SCA within a joint force to coordinate joint space operations and integrate space capabilities. The SCA has primary responsibility for joint space operations planning, to include ascertaining space requirements within the joint force. The SCA gathers operational requirements that may be satisfied by space capabilities and facilitates the use of established processes by joint force staffs to plan and conduct space operations.

For further detailed discussion of SCA, see JP 3-14, Space Operations.

v. Conducting civil-military operations (CMO) when directed.

For further discussion of CMO, see JP 3-57, Civil-Military Operations.

3. Designating an Area of Operations

a. **AOs** are defined by the JFC for surface (land and maritime) forces. An AO does not typically encompass the entire operational area of the JFC, but should be large enough for the JFLCC to accomplish the mission and protect the forces or capabilities provided. The JFLCC establishes an operational framework for the AO that assigns responsibilities to subordinate land commanders and maximizes the operational capabilities of all subordinate elements.

b. **C2 in Operational Areas.** The JFLCC is the supported commander within the land AO designated by the JFC. Within the designated AO, the JFLCC has the authority to designate target priority, effects, and timing of fires in order to integrate and synchronize maneuver, fires, and interdiction.

(1) Synchronization of efforts within land AO with theater and/or JOA-wide operations is of particular importance. To facilitate synchronization, the JFC establishes priorities that will be executed throughout the JOA, including within the land force commander's AO. The joint force air component commander (JFACC) is normally the supported commander for the JFC's overall air effort, while land and maritime component commanders are supported commanders for efforts in their AOs.

(2) In coordination with the JFLCC, commanders designated by the JFC to execute theater and/or JOA-wide functions have the latitude to plan and execute these JFC prioritized operations within the land AO. Any commander executing such a mission within a land AO must coordinate the operation to avoid adverse effects and friendly fire. If those operations would have adverse impacts within the land AO, the commander assigned to execute the JOA-wide functions must readjust the plan, resolve the issue with the JFLCC, or consult with the JFC for resolution.

c. **The JFLCC may subdivide some or all of the assigned AO.** These subordinate commander AOs may be contiguous or noncontiguous depending on the JFLCC's assignments, missions, and objectives. When the JFLCC's subordinate commanders are assigned contiguous AOs, a shared **boundary** separates the tactical units assigned to those designated subordinate commanders. When subordinate commanders are assigned noncontiguous AOs, the tactical units assigned to those designated subordinate commanders do not share a common boundary. Operation JUST CAUSE, in Panama, and OEF, in Afghanistan, are examples of operations with noncontiguous AOs. The intervening area between land forces within the joint force land component AO remains the responsibility of the JFLCC. If the Army provides the JFLCC, then an **Army support area** may be established for the conduct of operations and security of theater-level troops. This Army support area may also be designated as part of the **joint security area (JSA).** Figure II-1 depicts an example of an AO for the joint force land component and subordinate commands with contiguous and noncontiguous AOs.

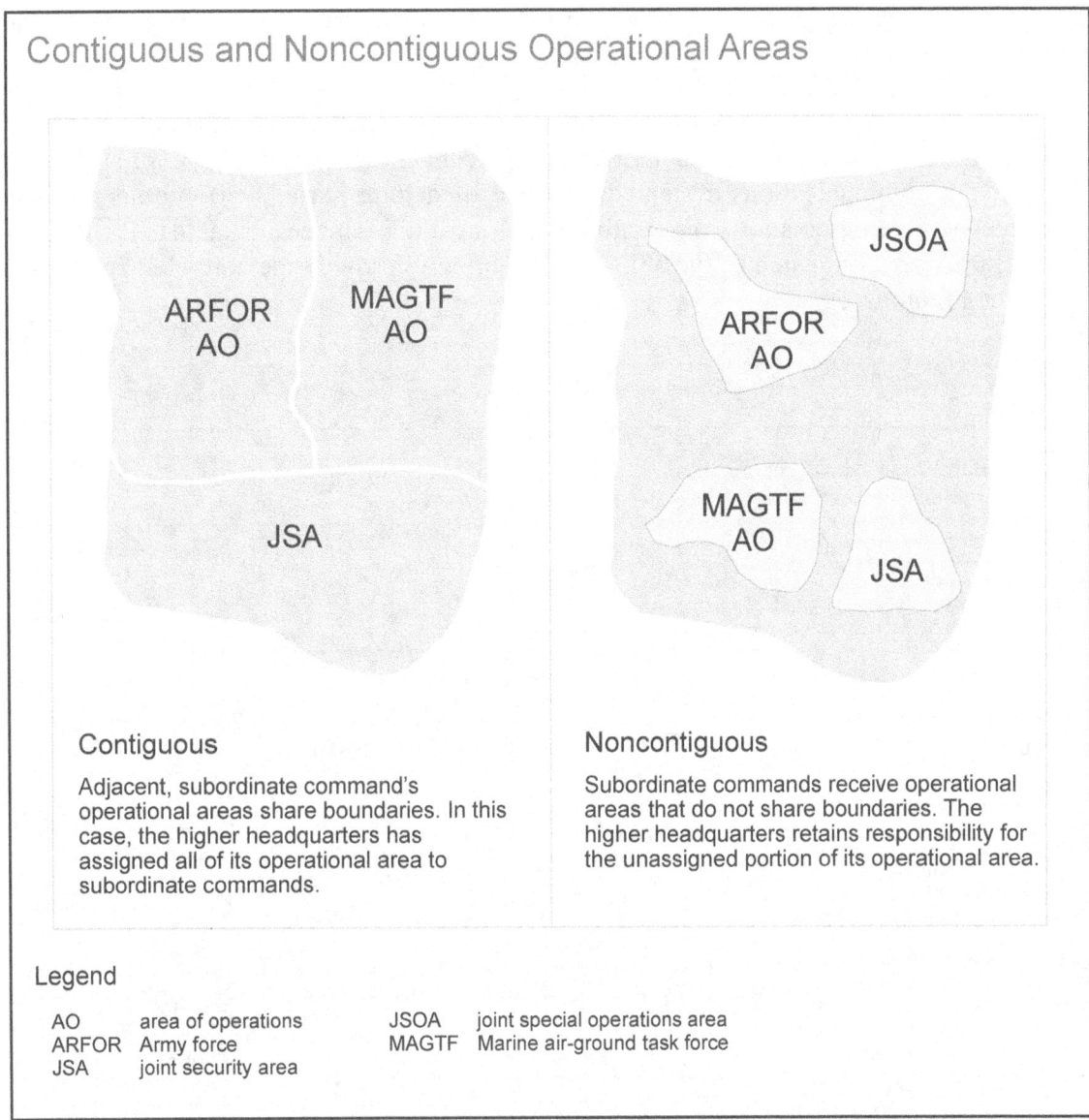

Figure II-1. Contiguous and Noncontiguous Operational Areas

See JP 3-0, Joint Operations, *and JP 3-02,* Amphibious Operations, *for more discussion on contiguous and noncontiguous operational areas.*

4. Organizing

a. The JFC establishing a functional component command has the authority to designate its commander. Normally, the Service component commander with the preponderance of forces to be tasked and the ability to C2 those forces will be designated as the functional component commander; however, the JFC will always consider the mission, nature, and duration of the operation, force capabilities, and the C2 capabilities in selecting a commander. In instances when the theater-level Service component commander is designated the JFLCC, the JFLCC normally delegates as many of the Service component related duties as practical to a subordinate ARFOR or Marine Corps forces (MARFOR) headquarters. These duties typically include Title 10, United States Code (USC) support and administrative control (ADCON) of Service forces.

b. Within the JFLCC headquarters, the commander, deputy commander, chief of staff, and key members of the staff (manpower and personnel directorate of a joint staff [J-1] through the communications system directorate of a joint staff [J-6]) should be fully integrated with representation from the forces and capabilities made available to the JFLCC. The commander designated as the JFLCC will normally provide the core elements of the staff (see Figure II-2).

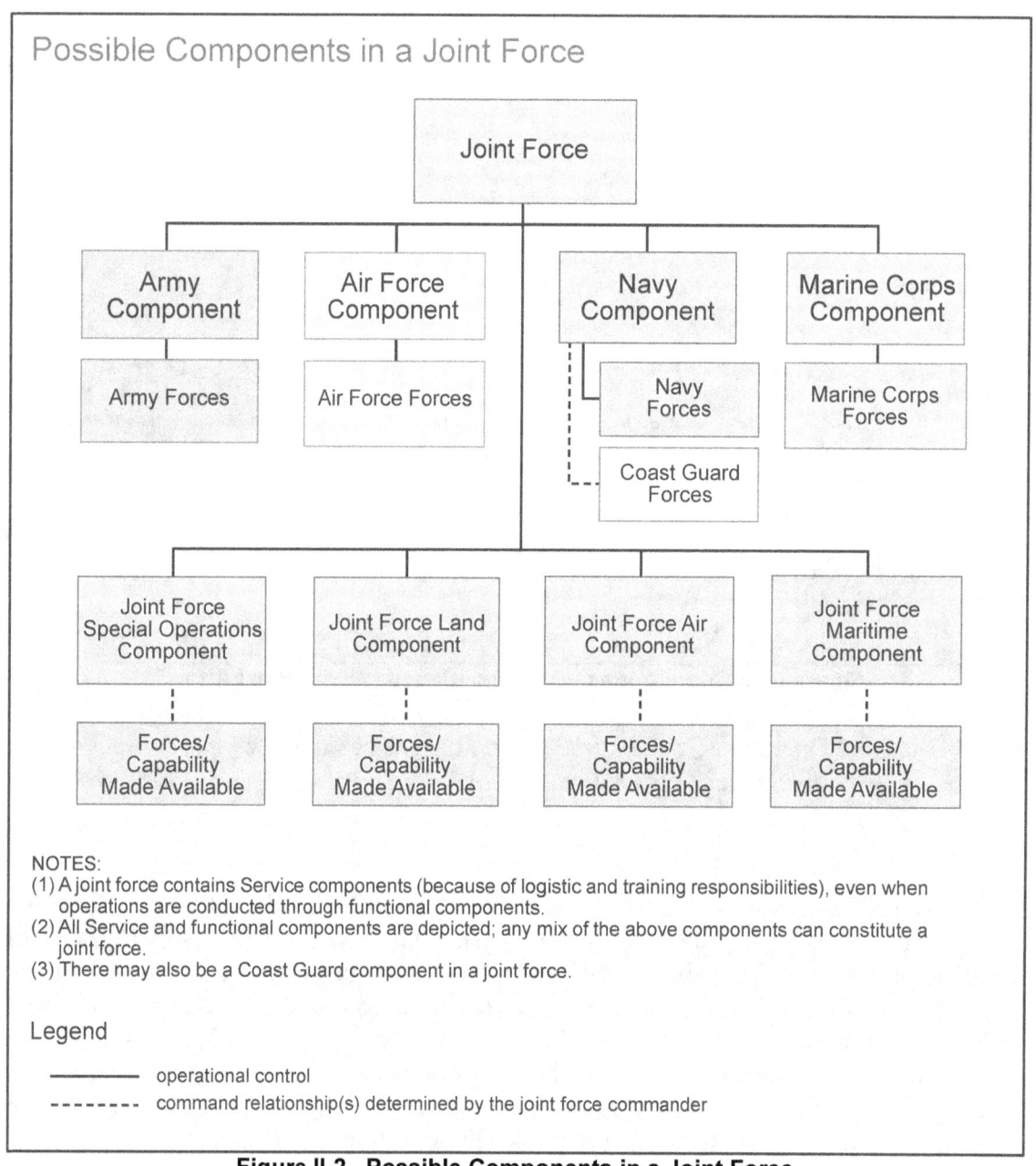

Figure II-2. Possible Components in a Joint Force

See JP 1-0, Joint Personnel Support, *and CJCSI 1301.01,* Joint Individual Augmentation Procedures.

c. **The forces required for the JFLCC to accomplish mission objectives are typically identified during planning and approved by the JFC.** The "Forces For" Assignment Tables, published annually in the Forces for Unified Commands Memorandum (odd-numbered years) and Global Force Management Implementation Guidance (even-numbered years), assign forces to the CCDR. Guidance for Employment of the Force and the Joint Strategic Capabilities Plan (JSCP) apportion major combat forces to CCDRs for planning. During crisis action planning, forces are allocated to CCDRs, and may differ from those apportioned during deliberate planning.

d. As the JFC develops the CONOPS, the Service and functional components develop their supporting plans. During this process, the JFC tasks the functional and Service components to provide estimates of forces required. **The JFLCC provides the force estimate in terms of capabilities required rather than specific units.** The JFC, working with the functional and Service components, sources the actual forces needed by the JFLCC. **Based upon JFC guidance, Service components designate specific units to report to the JFC, which are assigned a command relationship with the JFLCC.** After the forces are designated, the JFC plans and conducts the strategic deployment of forces. The JFLCC, like other functional component commanders, provides recommended phasing of required forces to the JFC. However, the JFLCC does not control the land force portion of the time-phased force and deployment data (TPFDD) or requests for forces (RFFs)/requests for capabilities (RFCs). Based on the Service and functional component recommendations, the JFC develops the integrated TPFDD or individual RFFs/RFCs and assigns required delivery dates.

For more information on TPFDD development, see Chairman of the Joint Chiefs of Staff Manual (CJCSM) 3122.01A, Joint Operation Planning and Execution System (JOPES), Volume I (Planning Policies and Procedures).

5. **Forming the Staff and Command Element**

a. **The JFLCC's staff should, by necessity, be composed of personnel from each Service and various Department of Defense (DOD) organizations and other supporting agencies. This provides the JFLCC with staff members who have the expertise and experience to assist in making informed decisions.** The JFLCC's staff is organized based upon the mission and forces assigned and attached. Because creating a new staff would be very time-consuming and inefficient, the staff organization will most likely be derived from an existing Service command structure. The most likely candidates for a JFLCC are Army corps or a Marine air-ground task force (MAGTF) (most likely a MEF). For smaller scale operations, a contingency command post from an ASCC, an Army division, or a Marine expeditionary brigade (MEB) could be employed. Ideally, the JFLCC and the deputy JFLCC or chief of staff would come from different Services. This construct should be replicated throughout the staff leadership to ensure an understanding of the distinct capabilities of each Service to optimize employment of the forces. Appendix A, "Notional Headquarters Organization," depicts a notional JFLCC's headquarters organization. The SOPs for the organization from which the JFLCC is designated normally form the baseline for the JFLCC's SOP.

b. The leader of each primary staff section provides staff supervision of the activities and capabilities associated with joint warfare at the operational level while providing expertise in the planning, execution, and assessment processes within their core functional areas. A primary staff section may be internally organized into six basic groups to reflect the following joint functions: movement and maneuver, intelligence, fires, sustainment, C2, and protection. The focused efforts of the primary staff officers in these core functions enable the commander and staff to maintain situational awareness and contributes to sound decision making during the course of the operation or campaign.

c. **Forming and Integrating the Joint Force Land Component Headquarters.** The headquarters are organized according to the JFC's implementing directive that establishes the roles and responsibilities of the JFLCC and designates the mission and forces assigned. **Normally, the staff will be built around the JFLCC's Service component staff and augmented with members of the other Service components or forces.** The JFLCC's staff should have key staff billets allocated such that all Services are appropriately represented and share equitably in staffing tasks. Key here is that these new members are not simply liaisons; they are part of the JFLCC's staff and ensure the synchronized execution of joint land operations. Forming the staff in advance, to facilitate training and exercising the integrated staff before conducting land operations, is critical to mission accomplishment.

(1) **Split Focus.** If the JFLCC retains Service component responsibilities for AOR-wide assigned same-Service forces, dual-hatting of the staff may burden some staff members with focus and time-management dilemmas. **The JFLCC obtains staff augmentation; splits his Service headquarters to establish dual command posts to provide exclusive focus on joint operational and Service administrative matters, respectively; or delegates all or many of the Service component-related tasks to a subordinate Service force headquarters.**

(2) **Staff Organization.** The JFLCC's staff, which will most likely be derived from an existing Service command structure, should be reasonably balanced as to numbers, experience, influence of position, and rank of the Service member concerned. Positions on the staff should be divided so that representation and influence generally reflect the Service composition of the force and the character of the contemplated operation; the number of personnel should be kept to the minimum consistent with the task to be performed. The JFLCC is authorized to organize the staff and assign responsibilities to individual Service members assigned to the staff as deemed necessary to accomplish the mission. See Appendix A, "Notional Headquarters Organization."

(a) **Traditional Arrangement. A joint staff arrangement normally is adopted** with directorates for manpower and personnel, intelligence, operations, logistics, plans, and communications systems forming the core. Optional directorates for IO, engineering, force structure and resource management, liaison officers (LNOs)/agency representatives, and **CMO** can be established depending on the nature of the operation, the operational environment, and the commander's desires.

(b) **Functional Arrangement. Alternatively, the staff may be organized into groups that reflect the joint functions of operational movement and maneuver, intelligence, fires, C2, protection, and sustainment.** The focused efforts of the staff in these functionally organized groupings may enable the JFLCC and senior staff to maintain a more logically integrated situational awareness across the operating systems, which contributes to sound decision making.

(3) **Forward Deployment.** At some point, a significant portion of the theater JFLCC's headquarters (depending on technological capabilities) may forward deploy to plan, coordinate, and conduct JRSOI and other joint land operations in the AO. The JFLCC normally will forward deploy as soon as the forward-deployed land component staff is operational. **It is critical for the JFLCC to get forward to conduct a personal assessment and interact with as many military, diplomatic, host nation (HN), and nongovernmental organization (NGO) officials in the AO as possible. Early arrival of the JFLCC also provides the personal opportunity to begin training a staff composed of many new players that will be conducting operational level tasks.**

d. **Joint Force Land Component Subordinate Elements.** The JFLCC controls and coordinates the joint land operations of all subordinate forces (see Figure II-3).

(1) **Multinational forces may be provided to the JFLCC for land operations.** Major concerns are command relationships and authorities, unity of effort, liaison requirements, intelligence and information sharing, integration of forces, interoperability of equipment, doctrine and procedures, language and cultural factors, mission assignment, AOs, rules of engagement (ROE), logistic readiness and capabilities, and national direction. When operating as part of a multinational (alliance or coalition), military command should follow multinational doctrine and procedures ratified by the US. For doctrine and procedures not ratified by the US, commanders should evaluate and follow the multinational command's doctrine and procedures, where applicable and consistent with US law, regulations, and doctrine.

See JP 3-16, Multinational Operations, *for additional guidance on these concerns.*

(2) **Same-Service Forces.** The JFLCC as a Service component commander normally exercises operational control (OPCON) of same-Service forces through subordinate Service force commanders.

(3) **Other Service Forces.** The JFLCC will normally be delegated tactical control (TACON) of other Service forces. **The JFLCC and staff must understand the capabilities and limitations of other Service forces.** A MAGTF placed TACON to an Army provided JFLCC will normally include Marine tactical air assets. The MAGTF commander will retain OPCON of organic air assets. Consequently, **commanders should specifically address the issue of JFLCC employment of Marine tactical aviation (that is, independent functional component air operations) during planning.** The JFLCC also must be prepared to receive and coordinate with Navy expeditionary forces (e.g., riverine, explosive ordnance disposal [EOD], and naval construction force), the elements of a

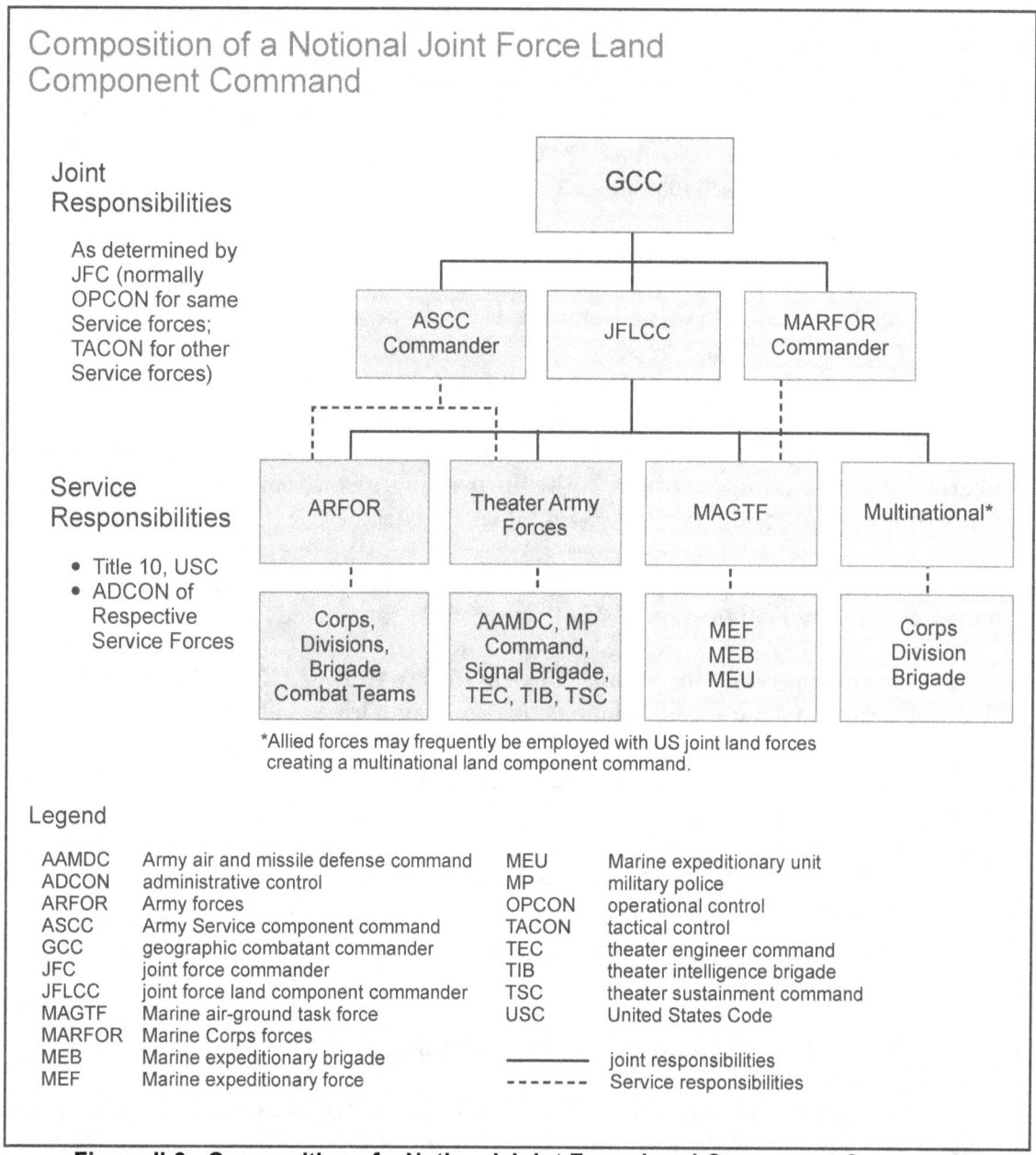

Figure II-3. Composition of a Notional Joint Force Land Component Command

maritime pre-positioning force (MPF) or the equipment of Army pre-positioned stocks (APS) when attached or provided.

See JP 1, Doctrine for the Armed Forces of the United States, *for more detail on joint C2.*

(4) **Specialized Ground Forces and Capabilities**

(a) US **Army Air and Missile Defense Command (AAMDC).** The JFLCC may employ an AAMDC to ensure that integrated AMD, to include ground based theater ballistic missile defense operations, conducted by land forces are planned, coordinated, and synchronized with the joint area AADP of the AADC. The AAMDC is normally also placed TACON to the AADC to ensure coordination.

(b) **Sustainment.** The authority to direct logistics is not normally resident in the JFLCC's command authority over other Service forces, unless the JFC delegates authority to the JFLCC for a common support capability or capabilities. If so designated, the JFLCC should establish a joint sustainment organization to manage land component common-user logistics (CUL) support. Army theater sustainment commands (TSCs) and expeditionary sustainment commands, as well as Marine logistics groups, may be suitable as a basis for augmentation to provide CUL.

For more information on authority for logistics common support capabilities, see JP 1, Doctrine for the Armed Forces of the United States, *and JP 4-0,* Joint Logistics.

(c) **Detainee Operations.** While this is an Army executive agent (EA) responsibility, the JFC may designate the JFLCC to supervise joint detainee operations of either enemy prisoners of war (EPWs) or civilian detainees. US Army military police commands or brigades can provide the basis for these organizations.

See JP 3-63, Detainee Operations, *for additional guidance on joint detainee operations.*

(d) **Engineering.** If warranted, a US Army theater engineer command (TEC) or engineer brigade may be provided to the JFLCC to supervise large scale engineering efforts in the JFLCC's AO. These units could be supplemented by either naval mobile construction battalions or US Air Force engineering squadrons. The TEC coordinates major construction planning and operations with the engineering staff section of a joint staff (J-7), when established, and receives planning and direction from the JFLCC's J-7.

For additional guidance on engineer doctrine for joint operations, see JP 3-34, Joint Engineer Operations.

(e) **Intelligence.** Specialized intelligence capabilities such as counterintelligence (CI), the use of unmanned systems, or joint interrogation and debriefing centers may be provided by the Army's theater intelligence brigade, other Service units, or national agencies.

For additional information on national level intelligence support, see JP 2-01, Joint and National Intelligence Support to Military Operations.

(f) **Joint Enabling Capabilities Command (JECC). United States Transportation Command's** JECC provides mission-tailored, joint capability packages to CCDRs to facilitate rapid establishment of joint force headquarters, fulfill global response force execution, and bridge joint operational requirements. JECC enables C2 at the operational level of war by providing alert-postured, expeditionary forces in three functional areas: joint planning; joint command, control, communications, and computer systems; and joint public affairs (PA). JECC can provide the JFC with forces from three subordinate commands: Joint Planning Support Element, with joint planners in five capability areas—plans, operations, intelligence, logistics, and information management; Joint

Communications Support Element, with rapidly deployable, en route, early entry, and scalable communications systems support capabilities; and Joint Public Affairs Support Element, with joint media and communications capable teams for enhanced, ready PA capability.

For a more detailed discussion of JECC, see JP 3-33, Joint Task Force Headquarters.

(g) **Standing Joint Force Headquarters – Elimination (SJFHQ-E).** United States Strategic Command may provide a SJFHQ-E for support of WMD elimination operations. SJFHQ-E provides a full-time, trained joint headquarters that can quickly integrate into strategic to operational level headquarters to provide WMD elimination expertise in planning, intelligence, and operations. It is a scalable, flexible, and deployable capability to support both deliberate and crisis planning for WMD elimination operations.

(h) **Other Capabilities.** The joint force land component may be augmented with forces, capabilities, and/or liaison from the Service and functional components of the joint force, Joint Staff, US Army Material Command, United States Transportation Command, United States Special Operations Command (USSOCOM), and Defense Logistics Agency. **These forces and capabilities will either be provided TACON, as supporting forces, or for coordination of specialized tasks and services.**

6. Liaison Requirements

a. **The JFLCC's liaison requirements include, as a minimum, liaison with other components of the joint force, either functional or Service.** The commander may require additional liaison with other organizations such as joint force headquarters, major subordinate commands, and multinational land forces not assigned to the command. The liaison teams or individuals represent the sending commander to the gaining commander and staff.

b. Command relationships and mission accomplishment influence LNO requirements. Liaison between the LCC and other organizations (i.e., functional/Service components, other United States Government [USG] departments and agencies, intergovernmental organizations [IGOs], and NGOs) is an important consideration when determining manning requirements within the JFLCC's staff. LNOs provide continuous and close liaison to facilitate unity of effort and accomplishment of JFC objectives. The JFLCC's battlefield coordination detachment (BCD) may represent the JFLCC at various meetings of joint force and component cross-functional staff organizations. **Examples include an air component coordination element (ACCE), (joint air component coordination element [JACCE] if provided by the JFACC), Army digital liaison detachments (DLDs), Marine air/naval gunfire liaison companies, and the BCD.** The JFACC establishes a JACCE or if a JFACC is not established; the commander, Air Force forces establishes an ACCE to interface and provide liaison with the JFLCC. The ACCE (or JACCE) assists the JFLCC's staff in planning air supporting and support requirements. The ACCE (or JACCE) interface includes exchanging current intelligence and operational data, support requirements, coordinating the integration of requirements for airspace control measures, joint fire support coordination measures (FSCMs), coordinated use of unmanned aircraft systems, and close air support

(CAS). The ACCE (or JACCE) is not an air support operations center or tactical air control party but can perform many air support planning functions. The BCD is an Army liaison provided by the Army component or force commander to the designated air operations center and/or to the component designated by the JFC to assist in planning, coordinating, and integrating joint air operations. The BCD processes Army requests for air support, monitors and interprets the land battle situation for the designated air operations center, and provides the necessary interface for exchange of current intelligence and operational data.

See JP 3-33, Joint Task Force Headquarters, *and JP 3-30,* Command and Control for Joint Air Operations, *for detailed information on liaison functions.*

SECTION B. COMMAND AND CONTROL

7. Functional Component Command Authority

Functional component commanders perform operational missions with authority delegated by the establishing JFC, who may be a CCDR or a subordinate JFC. **Functional components have specific delegated authority over forces or capabilities made available to them, but this does not affect the command relationships between Service component commanders and the JFC. Normally, these specific authorities are described in an establishing directive or "terms of reference" document prepared by the JFC staff.** (Note: Functional component commanders are component commanders of a joint force and do not constitute a "joint force command" with the authorities and responsibilities of a JFC, even when composed of forces from two or more Military Departments.)

See JP 1, Doctrine for the Armed Forces of the United States, *for additional information on functional component commands.*

8. Joint Security Area Responsibilities

a. **The JFLCC may be designated as the JSC by the JFC.** The JSC coordinates the overall protection of the JSA(s) among the component commanders in accordance with JFC directives and priorities. The JSC is also responsible for ensuring that the surface area requirements and priorities for the JSA are integrated in the overall security requirements of the joint force and are coordinated with the AADC who is responsible for defending the airspace over the operational area.

b. The JSC will typically establish a **joint security coordination center.** The staff of this center may be part of the JFLCC's headquarters or this function may be delegated to a subordinate unit, and will normally include representatives from all components operating in the JSA to assist in meeting joint security requirements. US Army maneuver enhancement brigades are suitable for this function.

See JP 3-10, Joint Security Operations in Theater, *and Army Doctrine Publication (ADP) 3-37,* Protection, *and Army Doctrine Reference Publication (ADRP) 3-37,* Protection.

9. Command Relationships

Unity of command and effort are primary considerations when designating a JFLCC. Use of the JFLCC is a JFC option for managing the operations of land forces and reducing the requirement for the JFC to oversee every task, thereby allowing the JFC to focus more on the overall joint operation or campaign. The JFLCC must understand the relationship with the JFC, the other components (Service and functional), and the forces and capabilities made available. **The JFLCC may provide support to other components and may similarly receive support from other Service or functional components.**

a. The JFC establishes the command relationships and assignment of forces to accomplish mission objectives. The JFC will also specify the command relationships between the functional components and Service components.

b. **The JFLCC is responsible for joint land operations as assigned and establishes command relationships for subordinate forces to the limits established by the JFC in his command relationship.** The JFLCC is responsible for planning and executing the land operations portion of the JFC's operation or campaign plan. The JFLCC prepares a supporting plan or order to the JFC's OPLAN that provides JFLCC's intentions, CONOPS, and details. The JFLCC directs current land operations while continuing to plan and prepare for future land operations.

(1) **Command Relationships with the JFC. The JFLCC reports directly to the JFC and advises the JFC on the proper employment of land forces assigned, attached, or made available.** The JFC has the authority to **assign** missions, redirect efforts, and direct coordination among subordinate commanders. JFCs should allow Service tactical and operational assets and groupings to function generally as they were designed. The intent is to meet the needs of the JFC while maintaining the tactical and operational integrity of the Service organizations.

(2) **Command Relationships Among Components.** The JFC may also establish support relationships among components. There are four defined categories of support that a JFC may direct over assigned or attached forces to ensure the appropriate level of support is provided to accomplish mission objectives. These are **general support, mutual support, direct support,** and **close support.** The establishing directive will specify the type and extent of support the specified forces are to provide. **The JFC determines not only how to organize the joint force into components, but also how each component relates to the others.** Support relationships afford an effective means to ensure unity of effort of various operations, each component typically receiving and providing support at the same time. The effectiveness of these support relationships depends on the establishment of personal trust and confidence between the respective component commanders that ensure mutual support even when not tasked.

(3) **Functional Component Supporting and Supported Relationships. The JFLCC will be the supported commander for operations conducted within the AO when designated by the JFC and may be the supporting commander for some functions.** Similar relationships can be established among all functional and Service

component commanders, such as the coordination of operations in depth involving the JFLCC and the JFACC or joint force special operations component commander (JFSOCC). The JFC's need for unified action dictates these relationships. Close coordination with the JFACC/AADC is necessary when the JFLCC provides joint suppression of enemy air defenses; provides attack operations against missile sites, airfields, C2, and infrastructure; or conducts land operations in the vicinity of a joint special operations area. To this end, the JFLCC will normally share the land COP with other JTF component commanders to meet the JTF's reporting criteria for a COP of the JOA as outlined in applicable JFC directives and amplifying instructions.

(4) **Command Relationships with Forces Made Available.** The JFLCC will normally be a Service component commander. **As Service component commander, the JFLCC normally exercises OPCON over its respective Service forces. As a functional component commander, the JFLCC normally exercises TACON over other forces or capabilities made available for tasking, or receives support as determined by the JFC.**

(a) Once the JFLCC is designated and forces are made available, the operational requirements of subordinate commanders are prioritized and presented to the JFLCC. However, Service component commanders remain responsible for their Military Department Title 10, USC, ADCON responsibilities, such as logistic and personnel services support, casualty operations, training, and Service intelligence operations.

(b) The JFLCC collaborates with other components and can receive and integrate component liaison teams to facilitate support and to coordinate the planning and execution of assigned land operations.

See JP 1, Doctrine for the Armed Forces of the United States, *for more on command and support relationships; for further detail on Title 10, USC, responsibilities, refer to Title 10, USC, Service responsibilities, and Department of Defense Directive (DODD) 5100.01,* Functions of the Department of Defense and its Major Components.

(5) **MPF Considerations**

(a) An MPF enables operations across the range of military operations and through any phase. When combined with the forces and their equipment arriving in the fly-in echelon, pre-positioning programs provide forward-deployed equipment and supplies needed to sustain a MEB-sized MAGTF for 30 days of operations, thus reducing total strategic lift requirements. Close coordination is required between a MAGTF and JFLCC's staff during an MPF operation.

(b) An MPF provides rapid response to regional contingencies and consists of the maritime pre-positioning ship squadron, Navy support element, and MAGTF. **An MPF is an option for the deployment of land forces made available to a JFLCC.** The MPF will be assigned to a functional or Service component commander as appropriate and perhaps based on the phase of the operation. **There is no single formula to incorporate an MPF into a naval, joint, or multinational effort;** organization depends on mission, force capabilities, tactical situation, and phase of the operations.

(c) The MAGTF commander's mission becomes the basis for all further MPF operation planning and must support the JFC's overall objectives. The landing force's CONOPS ashore is derived from the assigned mission. The JFLCC must be prepared to receive and integrate planning and liaison personnel from both the MAGTF commander and the commander, MPF. Without this close coordination between the JFLCC and MPF staffs, the MAGTF may not be able to effectively influence the land battle upon completion of the arrival and assembly phase of the MPF operation. Once the MAGTF commander reports that all essential elements of the MAGTF are combat ready, the establishing authority terminates the MPF operation and the MAGTF commander executes the assigned mission.

See also Navy Warfare Publication (NWP) 3-02.3M/Marine Corps Warfighting Publication (MCWP) 3-32, Maritime Pre-Positioning Force (MPF) Operations.

(6) **APS Considerations**

(a) APS is the expanded reserve of equipment for Army brigade combat teams (BCTs), theater-opening units, port-opening capabilities, and sustainment stocks forward deployed ashore or aboard ships. APS operations require airlift of an Army BCT with logistic support elements into a theater to link up with its equipment and supplies positioned ashore or aboard Army strategic flotilla ships. Their purposes are listed below:

1. To project to selected forward strategic locations early in a crisis an armored BCT that is capable of complementing other early arriving forces.

2. To project an afloat infantry BCT or supporting elements to a port to rapidly reinforce a lodgment established by Army early-entry forces and/or by amphibious assault elements, such as an Army airborne BCT or a MAGTF.

3. To protect key objectives.

4. To commence port operations to support the introduction of follow-on forces.

5. To rapidly provide a BCT or other capabilities to be prepared to conduct subsequent operations across the range of military operations.

(b) During preparation for APS operations, an initiating directive from higher authority will specify the command relationships. The **theater army commander**—the senior Army operational-level commander assigned to a combatant command—is responsible for planning APS operations. Thus, a theater army commander and staff must plan in detail the task organization and activities for each phase of the operation to ensure minimal disruption of C2 during phase transition. The theater army commander will designate which BCTs participate in the APS program, and make recommendations for their employment to the JFC. **Upon completion of reception, staging, onward movement and integration (RSOI), the BCT will be provided to a JFC, who may assign the BCT to a JFLCC.** As with the MPF, the JFLCC must receive and integrate planners and liaison personnel.

(c) APS employment focuses on expeditious deployment, assembly, and employment of BCTs and other enabling capabilities to meet the supported commander's requirements. It may also include tasks in support of other operations in the objective area. The mission order usually delineates the general AO, the required tasks of the BCT or other Army elements, the general time period for the deployment, required time for operational capability, time constraints on deployment operations—for example, availability of aircraft—and the estimated duration of operations.

See also Field Manual (FM) 3-35.1, Army Pre-Positioned Operations.

10. Functional Command Relationships

a. Command relationships between Service and/or functional component commands are established by the JFC. Joint interdependence is established by the commander through the deliberate assignment of command relationships with clear areas of operations, delegated authorities, and assigned responsibilities to best integrate the capabilities of the joint force. Elements of the different Services may be placed TACON or OPCON to functional component commands while retaining an ADCON relationship with their respective Service component commander. However, supported/supporting relationships may also be used to provide the necessary authority and basis for interdependence in the operational environment.

b. The Navy component commander normally establishes a subordinate TF comprised of forward Navy Expeditionary Combat Command (NECC) elements. These elements may consist of coastal riverine forces, naval mobile construction battalions, and Navy expeditionary logistics units operating ashore. This TF interfaces with and provides liaison to the JFLCC. The NECC LNO assists the JFLCC staff in planning naval supporting and support requirements. The NECC LNO exchanges current intelligence and operational data and coordinates planning requirements, to include coordinating airspace control measures, FSCMs, and CAS. A DLD may be used to provide ARFOR/JFLCC liaison to the Navy Service component commander/ joint force maritime component commander (JFMCC) and is responsible for synchronizing ground operations with joint maritime operations.

See JP 1, Doctrine for the Armed Forces of the United States, *for more information on functional command relationships.*

11. Cross-Functional Staff Organizations

a. **The JFLCC may be required to establish a variety of cross-functional staff organizations and send representatives to the JFC's and other component cross-functional staff organizations (see Figure II-4).**

For additional guidance on cross-functional staff organization, see JP 3-33, Joint Task Force Headquarters.

b. How JFLCC interfaces with other joint force C2 mechanisms is described in Figure II-5. Some considerations by type are:

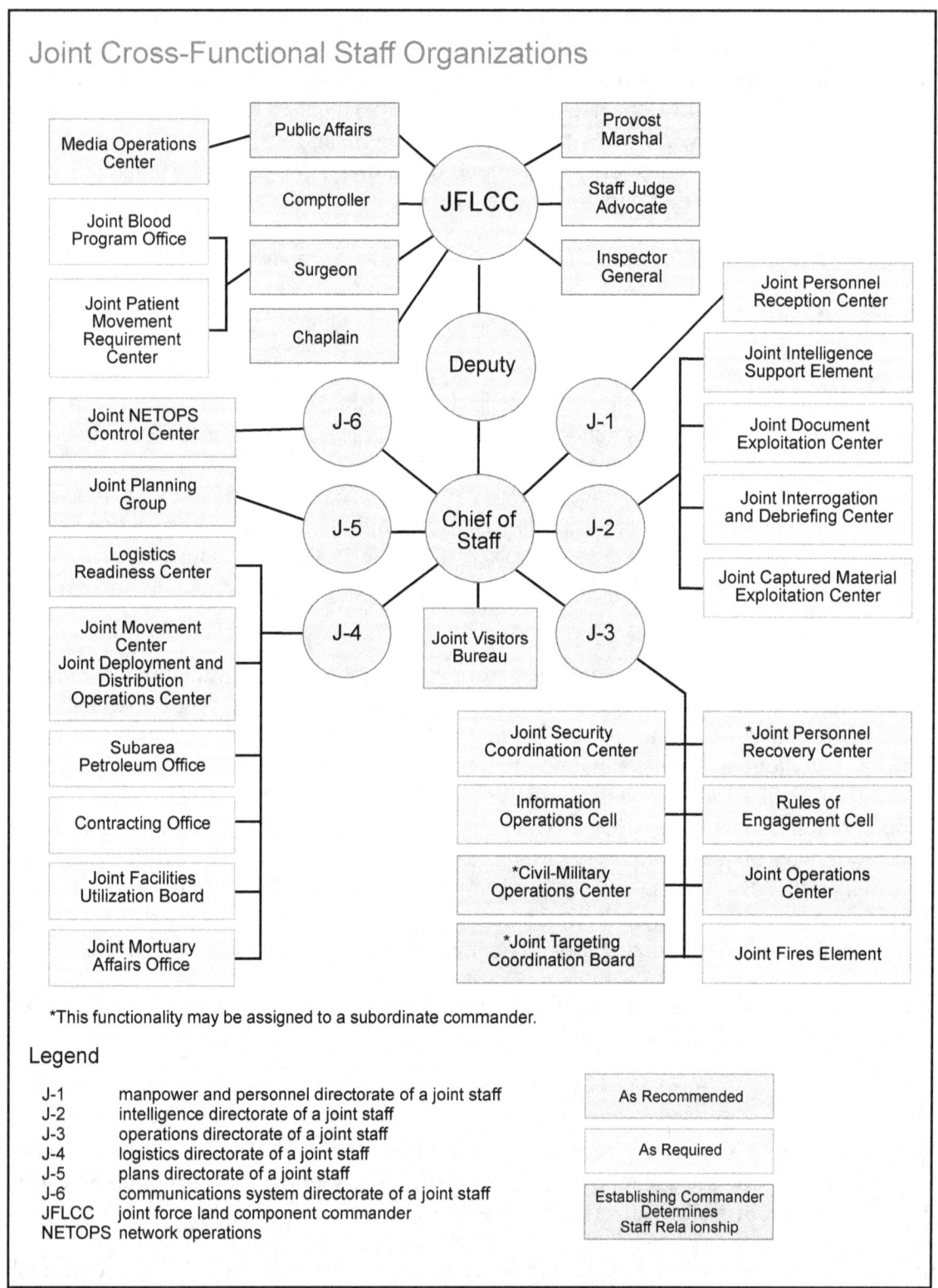

Figure II-4. Joint Cross-Functional Staff Organizations

Joint Force Land Component Commander Interface With Other Joint Force Command and Control Mechanisms

C2 Mechanism	Role/Function	JFLCC Interface
JFC's JTCB	Meets daily to provide broad targeting oversight functions that may include but are not limited to coordinating targeting information, providing targeting guidance and priorities, and refining the JIPTL.	JFLCC's representative attends JTCB meetings to represent land component interests. JFLCC's targeting coordination board provides input.
JFC's JPG	Meets daily or as required to conduct crisis action planning (to include course of action development and refinement), coordination of joint force operation order development, and planning for future operations (e.g., transition, termination, follow-on).	JFLCC's representative participates in all planning activities.
JFC's Joint Intelligence Operation Center	An interdependent, operational intelligence organization at the combatant command or joint task force (if established) level, that is integrated with national intelligence centers, and capable of accessing all sources of intelligence impacting military operations planning, execution, and assessment.	JFLCC's J-2 and staff maintain daily communication to provide, request, and receive intelligence products as needed.
JFC's Information Operations Cell	Meets daily or as required to integrate and synchronize information-related capabilities with other elements of the operation plan.	JFLCC's representative participates and coordinates with the JFLCC's JPG representative and other staff members.
JFC's Joint Transportation Board	Communicates JFC's priorities and adjudicates competing requirements for intratheater lift assets and helps resolve other issues that negatively impact the Defense Transportation System.	JFLCC's representative participates.
JFC's Joint Movement Center	Coordinates the employment of all means of transportation (including that provided by allies or host nations) daily to support the concept of operations.	JFLCC's representative participates.
JFC's Joint Petroleum Office	Plans and manages wholesale theater bulk petroleum support and develops the petroleum logistic support plan.	JFLCC's logistics directorate (J-4) coordinates and provides assistance as needed.
JFC's Civil-Military Operations Center	Meets daily and will coordinate all civil-military operations among other USG departments and agencies, intergovernmental organizations, nongovernmental organizations, coalition, and host nation members; and plays an integration and synchronization role with other elements of the operation plan.	JFLCC's representative participates.
JFACC's Targeting Effects Team	Processes all potential targets to balance component priorities with the JFC's objectives. Competing concerns are priorities against available assets to produce the JIPTL, apportionment recommendations, and close air support allocation.	BCD provides input and participates, coordinates with MARLE. MARLE provides input and participates, coordinates with BCD.
JFACC's ATO Development Processes	Produces a tasking document transmitted to components, subordinate units, and C2 agencies on projected sorties, capabilities, and/or forces to targets and specific missions. The ATO normally provides specific instructions to include call signs, targets, controlling agencies, etc., as well as general instructions.	BCD provides input and participates, coordinates with MARLE. MARLE provides input and participates, coordinates with BCD.
Airspace Control Authority ACO Development Process	Produces an ACO transmitted to components, subordinate units, and C2 agencies on joint use of the airspace. The ACO normally provides specific instructions for airspace deconfliction by time, altitude, or routes as well as general instructions.	BCD provides input and participates. Marine Direct Air Support Center provides input and participates. Army Theater Air Operations Group provides input and participates.

Joint Force Land Component Commander Interface With Other Joint Force Command and Control Mechanisms		
C2 Mechanism	**Role/Function**	**JFLCC Interface**
JSCC	Coordinates and oversees overall security operations within the AOR/JOA. Monitors emergency service, force protection, antiterrorism, physical security, and base and base cluster plans.	Joint security coordinator is the designated principal staff officer for the planning of joint security operations throughout the AOR/JOA.
Joint LOC Security Board	Assesses and reports LOC status and security capability shortfalls.	JSCC lead (or operations directorate of a joint staff [J-3]). Transportation representative. J-2 representative. Provost marshal office representative.
Joint Deployment and Distribution Operations Center	A combatant command movement control organization designed to synchronize and optimize national and theater multimodal resources for deployment, distribution, and sustainment.	
Joint Interagency Coordination Group	Interagency staff group that establishes regular, timely, collaborative working relationship between civilian and military with the capability to coordinate with other agencies.	JFLCC's representative participates. USG agencies and departments.
JFC's Joint Cyberspace Center	Combines input from United States Cyber Command and combatant commands to provide a regional/functional cyberspace situation awareness/common operational picture. Facilitates the coordination and deconfliction of combatant commander directed cyberspace operations.	JFLCC's representative participates to provide/request cyberspace operations products.
Legend		
ACO	airspace control order	JIPTL	joint integrated prioritized target list
AOR	area of responsibility	JOA	joint operations area
ATO	air tasking order	JPG	joint planning group
BCD	battlefield coordination detachment	JSCC	joint security coordination center
C2	command and control	JTCB	joint targeting coordination board
J-2	intelligence directorate of a joint staff	LOC	line of communications
JFACC	joint force air component commander	MARLE	Marine liaison element
JFC	joint force commander	USG	United States Government
JFLCC	joint force land component commander		

Figure II-5. Joint Force Land Component Commander Interface with Other Joint Force Command and Control Mechanisms

(1) **Planning.** Provide representation in the JFC's joint planning group (JPG) (or equivalent). Participate in the JFC's time-phased force and deployment list (TPFDL) development. Provide inputs into the JFC-approved joint AADP and the ACP.

(2) **Intelligence.** Provide appropriate intelligence support, including target intelligence packages, to the other joint force components and the joint targeting coordination board (JTCB). Provide and receive support from the theater joint intelligence operations center. Actively work to satisfy the JFC's priority intelligence requirements.

c. **Operations**

(1) Provide representation in the JFC's **JTCB and IO cell.** These representatives advocate the JFLCC's desired results/target nominations in the respective board or cell meetings. This should include participation in the JFC's assessment process.

(2) Develop IO requirements and the associated measures of effectiveness (MOEs) during the planning process. **These capabilities and processes must address the entire depth of the operation or campaign and are critical to shaping the operational environment before, during, and after operations.** MOEs required to assess the effects of a range of IRCs and operations may be resource intensive (polling, for example), and the related resource requirements must be introduced early for JFC validation and force provider planning.

(3) The **BCD,** Navy liaison element, and Marine liaison element members will participate in the JFACC's **targeting effects team and air tasking order (ATO) development processes**.

(4) The IO cell and cyberspace support element works with the JFLCC and key components of the JFLCC's staff to determine the cyberspace component of the JFLCC's defended asset list (DAL). Once the DAL has been determined, the IO cell and cyberspace support element focuses available capabilities to safeguard DAL assets.

d. **Sustainment.** Participation by the JFLCC's sustainment elements (logistic, personnel, financial management, etc.) in the JFC's pertinent boards or centers is critical. The **key logistics higher-level boards and centers are the theater-joint transportation board (T-JTB), joint deployment and distribution operations center (JDDOC), and joint movement center (JMC).**

e. **Engineer Boards, Centers, and Cells.** If an engineer staff is formed under the JFLCC, the following boards and cell may be established: a joint civil-military engineer board, a joint facilities utilization board, a joint environmental management board, and an explosive hazards coordination cell.

12. Interorganizational Coordination

a. **General.** JFLCCs are likely to operate with other USG departments and agencies, foreign governments, NGOs, IGOs, and the private sector in a variety of circumstances. The nature of interorganizational coordination demands that commanders and joint planners consider all instruments of national power and recognize which agencies are best qualified to employ these elements toward the objective. Other agencies may provide the lead effort during some operations, with DOD providing support; however, US military forces will remain under the DOD command structure while supporting other agencies. In some cases, a federal agency with lead responsibility is prescribed by law or regulation, or by agreement between the agencies involved.

b. **Civil-Military Integration.** The increasing complexity of peacekeeping and stability operations requires complete civil-military integration within the joint force land component. Presidential directives guide participation by all US civilian and military agencies in such operations. Military leaders must work with the other members of the national security team in the most skilled, tactful, and persistent ways to promote unified action; this is made more challenging by the agencies' different and sometimes conflicting policies, procedures, and decision-making processes. **Integration and coordination among** the military force and other USG departments and agencies, NGOs, IGOs, and the private sector is distinctly different from military C2. Military operations depend upon a command structure that is often very different from that of civilian organizations. These differences may present significant challenges to coordination. Military leaders must work with other members of the national security team to promote unified action. In the absence of a formal command structure, JFLCCs may be required to build consensus for effective unified action to achieve unity of effort. Robust liaison facilitates understanding, coordination, and mission accomplishment. This function is normally performed by the civil-military operations directorate of a joint staff (J-9) or senior civil affairs (CA) representative supporting the JFLCC. The JFC may direct the establishment of a civil-military operations center (CMOC) to enhance the integration of civil and military efforts.

c. **Formal Agreements.** Formal agreements such as memoranda of understanding or terms of reference are more common among military organizations and other USG departments and agencies or HNs than between military organizations and NGOs. Although formal agreements may be established, commanders should not expect that formal agreements with NGOs exist. Heads of agencies or organizations and specifically authorized military commanders negotiate and cosign these agreements.

d. **Information Sharing.** Unified action requires effective information sharing among DOD, other USG departments and agencies, and state and local agencies. Accordingly, JFLCCs should develop habitual relationships, procedures, and agreements with the individual agencies. For example, DOD support to homeland security requires detailed coordination and information sharing with the Department of Homeland Security (DHS). Implementation of a collaborative information environment (CIE) that connects commanders and these various organizations, using commonly accessible portals and collaborative tools, provides a proven means for effective coordination and information sharing.

CJCSM 6715.01, Joint Operational Employment of Virtual Collaboration, *provides further information on the means for CIE implementation.*

e. **Joint Interagency Coordination Group (JIACG).** The JIACG, an element of a CCDR's staff, is an interagency staff group that establishes regular, timely, and collaborative working relationships between civilians and military operational planners at the combatant commands. There is currently no standardized structure for the JIACG. It should include USG civilian and military experts accredited to the CCDR and tailored to meet the requirements of a supported combatant command. The JIACGs complement the interagency coordination that takes place at the strategic level through DOD and the National Security Council System. JIACG members participate in deliberate, crisis action, security cooperation, and other operational planning. They provide a conduit back to their parent organizations to help synchronize joint operations with the efforts of other USG departments and agencies. If required, a JIACG may be formed at JFLCC level.

For additional guidance on JIACG, see JP 3-08, Interorganizational Coordination During Joint Operations.

f. **JFLCC Staff.** There are several other means available at the JFLCC level to conduct interagency coordination. This coordination can occur in the various boards, centers, cells, and/or working groups established within the LCC. The JFLCC and other USG departments and agencies also may agree to form steering groups to coordinate actions. In the case of a DOD directed DSCA mission, the JFLCC can establish a defense coordinating element to conduct direct coordination with the federal coordinating officer in the joint field office.

g. **CMOC.** One method to facilitate unified action and conduct on-site interagency coordination for CMO is for the commander to establish a CMOC. The CMOC is an organization established by the JFC, the core of which is normally comprised of CA forces, to plan or coordinate actions affecting the civil component of the operational environment and facilitate coordination and collaboration for attainment of regional or stability objectives through unity of effort. Through a structure such as a CMOC, the JFLCC can gain a greater understanding of the roles of IGOs and NGOs and how they influence mission accomplishment.

For additional guidance on CMOCs, see JP 3-57, Civil-Military Operations. *For additional guidance on interagency coordination, refer to JP 3-08,* Interorganizational Coordination During Joint Operations.

h. **Other Civil-Military Coordination Mechanisms.** To ensure thorough integration of cooperation between the military and other civilian organizations, the commander may require a number of other centers, including a humanitarian assistance coordination center, humanitarian operations center, humanitarian liaison center, and humanitarian assistance survey team. These centers all provide the commander a coordination point between military and various civilian partners.

13. Multinational Operations

a. To achieve the most effective C2 and best use the capabilities of the multinational land forces, **the multinational force commander normally designates a single LCC for land operations. Multinational forces** may be part of a coalition or an **alliance.** How that structure is organized will be based on the needs, political goals, constraints, and objectives of the participating nations. The multinational commander has the option of creating a land component command within either an alliance or coalition.

(1) In alliance operations, such as those conducted by NATO and the United Nations, there are normally existing land commands that can serve as an alliance LCC.

(2) In coalition operations, the multinational commander of the lead nation can establish a land component command from an existing command organization or through establishment of a new command made up of various command staffs.

b. In multinational operations, the multinational LCC considers many issues, with particular attention to the following:

(1) **Command Authority.** Higher authority and agreements with participating nations will determine the command authority over forces provided to the LCC. Unity of

effort must be a key consideration with the respective **national command elements,** or the senior element within a multinational command so designated to represent the national command channels from its individual nation. The multinational land staff must gain the trust of, have rapport with, have respect for, develop knowledge of, and have patience with all its partner nations. Liaison and coordination centers will enhance C2.

(2) **Information Exchange Requirements.** Information sharing, classification, and disclosure issues will require early planning and resolution, especially for any intelligence requirements. Information sharing, cooperation, collaboration, and coordination are enabled by an intelligence and information sharing environment that fully integrates joint, multinational, and interagency partners in a collaborative enterprise. The JFC participating in multinational operations tailors the policy and procedures for that particular operation based on national and theater guidance.

See JP 3-16, Multinational Operations, *for additional information on information sharing.*

(3) **Communications.** Varying degrees of technological capabilities may constrain activities and cause interoperability challenges. Countries equipped with older communications technologies will require secure communications systems and specially equipped LNO teams, such as Army DLDs, to support them. In other situations, US forces must be capable of interoperability even when the US is not the lead nation.

(4) **Integration of Forces.** Understanding the capabilities and limitations of multinational forces is essential to assigning missions and reducing friendly fire incidents. In addition, US joint land forces should be culturally prepared, to include obtaining language expertise, for working with multinational partners. Other USG departments and agencies must also work with multinational commands.

(5) **ROE.** Differing national laws and treaties will impact ROE. Obtaining concurrence for ROE from national authorities should be addressed early in the planning process and may require early resolution and consensus building. Differences in interpretations need to be reconciled as much as possible to develop and implement simple ROE that can be tailored by member forces to their national policies.

(6) **Logistics.** Although logistics is normally a responsibility of each contributing nation, economy of force considerations requires adaptability and planning with centralized control. Funding authorities should be identified early. Each nation should have a designated **national support element.** This is any national organization or activity that supports national forces that are a part of a multinational force. Their mission is nation-specific support to units and common support that is retained by that nation.

JP 3-16, Multinational Operations, *provides further information on multinational C2. See also JP 4-08,* Logistics in Support of Multinational Operations. *AJP 3.2,* Allied Joint Doctrine for Land Operations, *provides further information on the doctrine for planning, preparing, and executing NATO (alliance or coalition) land component operations.*

14. Communications Support Systems

The CCDR, through the JFC and functional/Service components, ensures effective, reliable, and secure communications system and cyberspace defense services are consistent with the overall joint campaign plan. As driven by the mission, the foundation of the communications system is laid by the C2 organization of forces assigned to the JFC.

a. The JFLCC provides standardized direction and guidance on communications systems matters to the JFLCC subordinate commanders and any other communications supporting elements, as these matters affect the operational mission. The JFLCC establishes communications systems and DODIN responsibilities for units assigned, attached, and forces made available for tasking. The Service component commands have the overall responsibility for providing communications systems and DODIN capabilities to their own forces unless otherwise directed. Providing communications hardware and software is a Service component responsibility.

b. The JFLCC utilizes existing theater communications systems that are established and managed by the GCC. Theater systems may need to be supplemented based on operational need. This provides theater-wide voice, data, and message connectivity between all components and elements. In addition, these systems and nonstandard commercial systems address unique communications connectivity requirements that provide for the appropriate interface between land forces and other components, and other USG departments and agencies, IGO, and NGO partners, and C2 integrated into a partner information sharing environment that permits timely execution of assigned missions. Among the systems the JFLCC should consider are any forms of CIE that may have been implemented by the JFC to afford interface of land forces with these traditional partners and which may extend even to nontraditional partners.

c. Communications are established as specified in the OPLAN and/or OPORD (generally found in annex K).

d. The J-6 provides functional expertise to the JFLCC concerning communications **systems** matters. The J-6 focuses on communications **systems** issues affecting joint land operations assigned to the JFLCC and has responsibility for achieving integration of those communications systems so as to assure their suitability for use by the JFLCC. Routine communications systems management is the responsibility of the JFC and the subordinate Service component commands. Appendix A, "Notional Headquarters Organization," provides additional information regarding the organization and responsibilities of the J-6 staff.

e. The intelligence directorate of a joint staff (J-2), operations directorate of a joint staff (J-3) and J-6 may establish a prioritized circuit restoration plan that includes preplanned responses, bandwidth reallocation, prevention of network intrusions, and recovery from data exchange bottlenecks, in order to meet the commander's critical information requirements (CCIRs).

See also JP 6-0, Joint Communications System, and JP 6-01, Joint Electromagnetic Spectrum Management Operations.

Intentionally Blank

"Lack of a Ground Component Commander was a mistake: even absent a combat ground offensive, the planning and staffing capabilities that an ARFOR [Army forces] would have provided were needed...significant ground planning responsibilities were shifted to the JTF [joint task force] staff – that was only marginally prepared to handle myriad issues pertaining to Initial Entry Force for Kosovo and TF [task force] FALCON."

Admiral James Ellis, Commander, Joint Task Force NOBLE ANVIL during Operation ALLIED FORCE in letter to RAND Corporation, December 2000

SECTION A. PLANNING

1. Strategic Planning Considerations

Planning for the employment of military forces is an inherent responsibility of command. Joint planning integrates military actions with those of other instruments of national power and our multinational partners in time, space, and purpose to attain a specified end state. Joint land force operational planning links the tactical employment of land forces to campaign and strategic objectives through the achievement of operational goals.

2. Range of Military Operations

a. **General.** The use of land force capabilities in **military engagement, security cooperation, and deterrence** activities shapes the operational environment and helps to keep the day-to-day tensions between nations or groups below the threshold of armed conflict while maintaining US global influence. Many of the missions associated with **crisis response and limited contingencies**, such as foreign humanitarian assistance (FHA), may not require land combat. But others, as evidenced by Operation RESTORE HOPE in Somalia, can be extremely dangerous and may require land operations to protect US and other forces while accomplishing the mission. **Major operations and campaigns** requiring significant land forces often contribute to a larger, long-term effort (e.g., OEF and OIF). The nature of the operational environment is such that the US land forces often will be engaged in several types of joint operations simultaneously. For these operations, commanders combine and sequence offensive, defensive, and stability missions and activities to achieve the objective. The commander for a particular operation determines the emphasis to be placed on each type of mission or activity.

See JP 1, Doctrine for the Armed Forces of the United States, *for more on the range of military operations.*

b. **Joint Land Operations in Major Operations and Campaigns**

(1) When required to achieve national strategic objectives or protect national interests, the **US national leadership may decide to conduct a major operation or**

campaign involving large-scale combat, placing the US in a wartime state. In such cases, the general goal is to **prevail** against the enemy as quickly as possible, conclude hostilities, and establish conditions favorable to the population and the US and its multinational partners. Establishing these conditions often requires conducting stability operations in support of broader stability, security, transition, and reconstruction efforts. While the Department of State (DOS) is the lead agent for stability and reconstruction efforts, stability operations is a core US military mission that helps to establish order and protect US interests and values. The immediate goal often is to provide the local populace with security, restore essential services, and meet humanitarian needs. The long-term goal is supporting DOS and the HN to develop indigenous capacity for securing essential services, operating a viable market economy, and maintaining rule of law, democratic institutions, and a robust civil society. This requires a coordinated approach with a chief of mission or other designated individual developing a country (and possible region/province specific) plan in conjunction with all participating agencies and controlling or coordinating all US activities in support of that plan.

(2) Ground combat—either offensive with the purpose of securing a vital area and destroying the adversary defending it, or defensive with the objective to deny a vital area to the adversary—is the most difficult and costly type of land operation. All aspects of ground combat that have historically extracted a terrible price on attacker, defender, and civilian alike remain present today, multiplied by the increased size and complexity of modern urban areas and increase in the number of inhabitants. However, other types of operations exist in war that may accomplish strategic and operational objectives without ground offensive combat. Aviation assets can destroy and disrupt adversary forces and functions and the infrastructure on which they depend. SOF can accomplish similar missions. Employment of IRCs aligned with strategic guidance can lessen popular support for adversary leaders, and/or decrease the ability of the adversary leader to effectively direct his forces. The use of nonlethal capabilities can assist ground forces and decrease the likelihood of civilian casualties. If ground combat operations are necessary, appropriate shaping of the operational environment and application of force may prevent full-scale combat. The JFC should consider forces and functions in unusual combinations and relations when conducting joint land operations, befitting the nature of the land operational environment.

c. **Joint Land Operations in Crisis Response and Limited Contingency Operations.** Crisis response and limited contingency operations conducted by US forces increasingly take place in urban areas. These operations can be conducted in a permissive, uncertain, or hostile environment. However, in many areas of the world stability is tenuous at best, making the threat of some types of hostile action real in nearly all operations. As in Somalia in the early 1990s, some crisis response and limited contingency operations began as purely humanitarian operations and ended in urban combat.

d. **Joint Land Operations in Military Engagement, Security Cooperation, and Deterrence.** These ongoing activities are conducted by GCCs to establish, shape, maintain, and refine relations with other nations within their AORs. They encompass a wide range of actions where the military instrument of national power is tasked to support other USG departments and agencies and cooperate with IGOs (e.g., United Nations, NATO) and other countries to protect and enhance national security interests, build partner capacity, and deter conflict. These operations usually involve a combination of military forces and capabilities, to include joint land forces, as well as the efforts of other USG departments and agencies, IGOs, and NGOs in a complementary fashion. DOS is frequently the federal agency with lead responsibility and nearly always is a principal player in these activities. Consequently, GCCs may employ their JFLCCs to conduct these operations and direct them to maintain a working relationship with the chiefs of the US diplomatic missions in their area. Land commanders and their staffs should also establish contact and maintain a dialogue with pertinent other USG departments and agencies, IGOs, and NGOs to share information and facilitate future joint land operations.

e. **Simultaneous Operations.** The nature of joint land operations often requires different types of operations to occur simultaneously or in rapid sequence, sometimes in close proximity. A situation can easily arise where members of the same friendly unit may at one moment be feeding and clothing dislocated civilians, at the next holding two warring tribes apart, and the next fighting a highly lethal battle—all within the same area. In a larger context, the joint force may have to conduct **FHA** and other operations at the same time and in the same area where **land operations** are taking place. Such action may not wait for the stabilize and enable civil authority phases, but may be an integral part of the overall **land operation.** In addition, joint land **operations will normally bring with it requirements normally associated** with noncombat **crisis response and limited contingency operations; crisis response and limited contingency operations may very well entail joint land operations.**

See JP 1, Doctrine for the Armed Forces of the United States.

3. **Support to Joint Operation Planning**

a. **General. JFLCC planning tasks are to:**

(1) Prepare and coordinate required land component OPLANs or OPORDs in support of assigned JFC missions.

(2) Coordinate land component planning efforts with higher, lower, adjacent, and multinational headquarters as required.

(3) Develop land component COAs within the framework of the JFC-assigned objectives or missions, forces available, and the commander's intent.

(4) Determine land component force requirements and coordinate land force planning in support of the selected COAs. The JFLCC conducts planning using the planning processes of the command that forms the core of the headquarters. While almost all headquarters use the planning cycle described in joint planning publications, the specific steps in the process may have different names and somewhat different activities. The JFLCC's staff, provided by Services other than the core of the headquarters and integrated into the core staff, must quickly adapt to the planning processes and battle rhythm of the staff they are joining.

b. The joint operation planning process (JOPP) is a proven analytical process that provides an orderly approach to planning at any point of joint operations. JOPP may be used by a JFLCC's staff during deliberate and crisis action planning. The focus of JOPP is the interaction for planning between commanders, staffs, and echelons. JOPP is also linked with the joint intelligence preparation of the operational environment (JIPOE). JIPOE is the analytical process used by joint intelligence organizations to produce intelligence assessments, estimates, and other intelligence products in support of the JFC's decision-making process. The process is used to analyze the physical domains; the information environment; political, military, economic, social, information, and infrastructure systems; and all other relevant aspects of the operational environment, and to determine an adversary's capabilities to operate within that environment.

See JP 2-01.3, Joint Intelligence Preparation of the Operational Environment, *and JP 5-0,* Joint Operation Planning, *for more information on JIPOE.*

c. **Commander's Operational Approach.** The JFLCC's planners must first frame the strategic and operational problem by developing an understanding of the situation before addressing operational design and ultimately OPLANs. Several cognitive models exist to assist JFLCC's and their staffs as they plan and execute joint land operations. The operational approach is the commander's visualization of how the operations should transform current conditions at end state.

(1) The operational approach is based largely on an understanding of the operational environment and the problem facing the JFLCC.

(2) Developing a commander's operational approach provides for *problem framing* as one method for establishing the context of a situation within which a commander and staff must act to achieve the strategic objectives. The essence of problem framing is to examine the problem from multiple perspectives and set conditions for learning about the problem throughout the planning and execution of military operations. Framing can also support the commander's discourse with superiors regarding the nature of the problem the commander has been asked to solve. It also assists in developing a mutual understanding of the operational environment.

(3) Operational design follows the commander's understanding of the situation and problem framing by applying operational art to the conception and construction of the framework that underpins an operation or campaign. The JFLCC, based upon experience, intuition, instincts, and advice from the staff and other external advisors, employs the creative aspects of operational design elements in a logical process that leads toward COA development.

d. **Operational Art.** **Operational art** is the application of creative imagination by commanders and staffs—supported by their skill, knowledge, and experience. Operational art integrates ends, ways, and means and considers risk across the levels of war. **Operational art determines when, where, and for what purpose major forces are employed and should influence the adversary disposition.** It governs the deployment of those forces, their commitment to or withdrawal from battle, and the arrangement of battles and major operations to achieve operational and strategic objectives. JFLCC operational planning addresses some activities required for conducting joint/multinational land operations. These activities are:

(1) Support the GCC's effort in conducting deterrence, shaping operations, theater security cooperation, and building partner capacity.

(2) Employment planning that describes how to set the theater and apply force to achieve specified military objectives.

(3) Sustainment planning which is directed toward providing and maintaining levels of personnel, materiel, and consumables required to sustain the levels of combat activity for the estimated duration and at the desired level of intensity.

(4) Deployment and redeployment planning that includes the development of the TPFDL, monitoring the force flow, and the redeployment of forces from theater at the end of the operation or campaign.

For more information on deployment and redeployment planning, see JP 3-35, Deployment and Redeployment Operations.

(5) Support the GCC's effort in conducting stability operations in all phases and planning for transitions during the operation or campaign.

(6) **Environmental Considerations.** Environmental considerations tied to risk management and the safety and health of Service members should be factored into all phases of joint land operations.

See JP 5-0, Joint Operation Planning, *ADP 5-0,* The Operations Process, *and MCWP 5-1,* Marine Corps Planning Process, *for more details on planning processes.*

e. **JPG.** The primary planning element for the JFLCC to support the JFC's planning or to perform component planning is the JPG. Planners from the JFLCC's core headquarters staff element are the nucleus around which the JPG is normally built. It includes personnel from each of the primary coordinating, functional, and special staff elements, LNOs, and when necessary, planners from the JFLCC's subordinate commands or multinational land forces (see Figure III-1). The JPG develops and disseminates staff planning guidance and schedules. It confirms the process and products to be developed and delivered to support the JFLCC's planning effort. The JPG is the planning hub and synchronization center for future plans. The JPG develops the CONOPS for each plan. The CONOPS describes how the actions of the joint land force and supporting organizations will be integrated, synchronized, and phased to accomplish the mission, including potential branches and sequels. Using **mission-type orders**, the JPG writes (or graphically portrays) it in sufficient detail so that subordinate and supporting commanders understand the **commander's intent,** purpose, and any specific tasks or requirements and can innovatively develop their supporting plans accordingly. During its development, the JPG determines the best arrangement of simultaneous and sequential actions and activities to create desired effects and accomplish the assigned mission consistent with the approved COA. This arrangement of actions

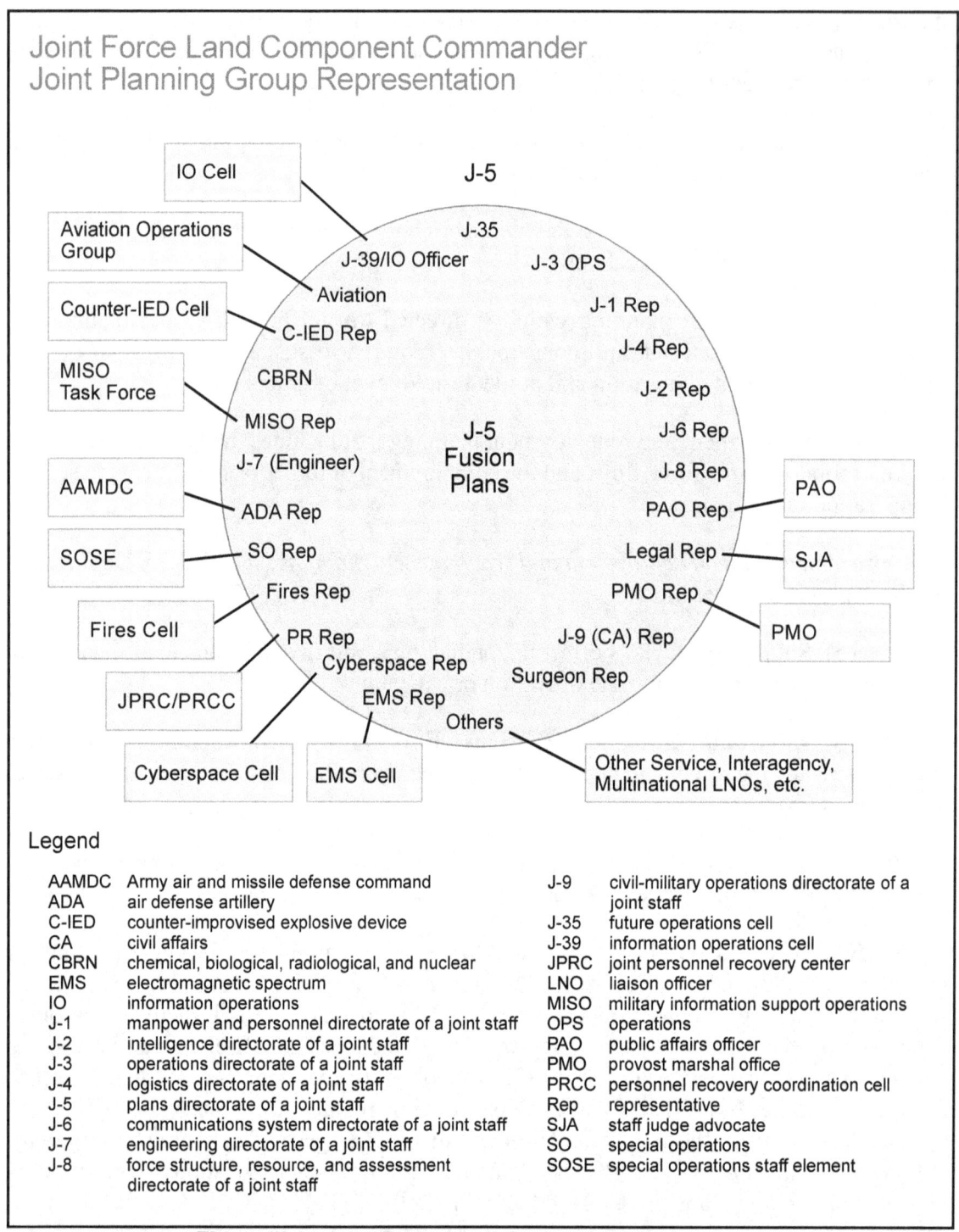

**Figure III-1. Joint Force Land Component Commander
Joint Planning Group Representation**

dictates the sequencing of forces into the operational area, providing the link between joint operation planning and force planning.

For a more detailed discussion of CONOPS development, see JP 5-0, Joint Operation Planning.

f. **Plans-Operations Relationship.** The JFLCC headquarters orients on three planning horizons: short, medium, and long. These correspond with current operations, future operations, and future plans. Upon completion of the planning products and orders, the JPG (future plans) organizes to conduct a plans transition. **Once plans are prepared and execution begins, the JPG focus shifts to planning "what's next" or sequels primarily with higher headquarters, while handing off the plan to the current J-3 for execution and preparation of all necessary fragmentary orders directing tactical action.** This requires an organizational procedure to transfer responsibilities and products from the long range planners to those operators responsible for execution. Key to the success of the plans transition is the requirement that the organization responsible for execution has enough resources, experience, and understanding of the plan to effectively execute it. Experience has shown that the current operations cell is often too immersed in ongoing operations to plan outside the current 24-hour period. This may require the organization of a separate future operations cell (J-35) for focusing on "what if" and branch plans development (see Figure III-2).

See JP 5-0, Joint Operation Planning, *for more information on planning horizons.*

g. **Phasing**

(1) **Purpose.** The purpose of phasing is to help the commander organize operations by integrating and synchronizing subordinate operations. Phasing is most directly related to the "arranging operations" and "lines of effort" elements of operational design. Phasing helps JFLCCs and staffs visualize and think through the entire operation or campaign and to define requirements in terms of forces, resources, time, space, and purpose. The primary benefit of phasing is that it assists commanders in systematically achieving military objectives that cannot be attained all at once by arranging smaller, related operations in a logical sequence. Phasing can be used to gain progressive advantages and assist in achieving objectives as quickly and effectively as possible. Phasing also provides a framework for assessing risk to portions of an operation or campaign, allowing development of plans to mitigate this risk.

(2) **Application.** The JFC's vision of how a campaign or operation should unfold drives subsequent decisions regarding phasing. Phasing, in turn, assists in framing commander's intent and assigning tasks to subordinate commanders. By arranging operations and activities into phases, the JFC can better integrate and synchronize the land component command's operations and other subordinate operations in time, space, and purpose. Each phase should represent a natural subdivision of the intermediate objectives of the operation or campaign. As such, a phase represents a definitive stage during which a large portion of the forces and joint/multinational capabilities are involved in similar or mutually supporting activities.

(3) **Number, Sequence, and Overlap.** Working within the phasing construct, the actual phases used will vary (compressed, expanded, or omitted entirely) with the joint operation and be determined by the JFC. During planning, the JFLCC may establish sub-phases and conditions, objectives, or events for transitioning from one sub-phase to another and plans sequels and branches for potential contingencies. Phases are designed and

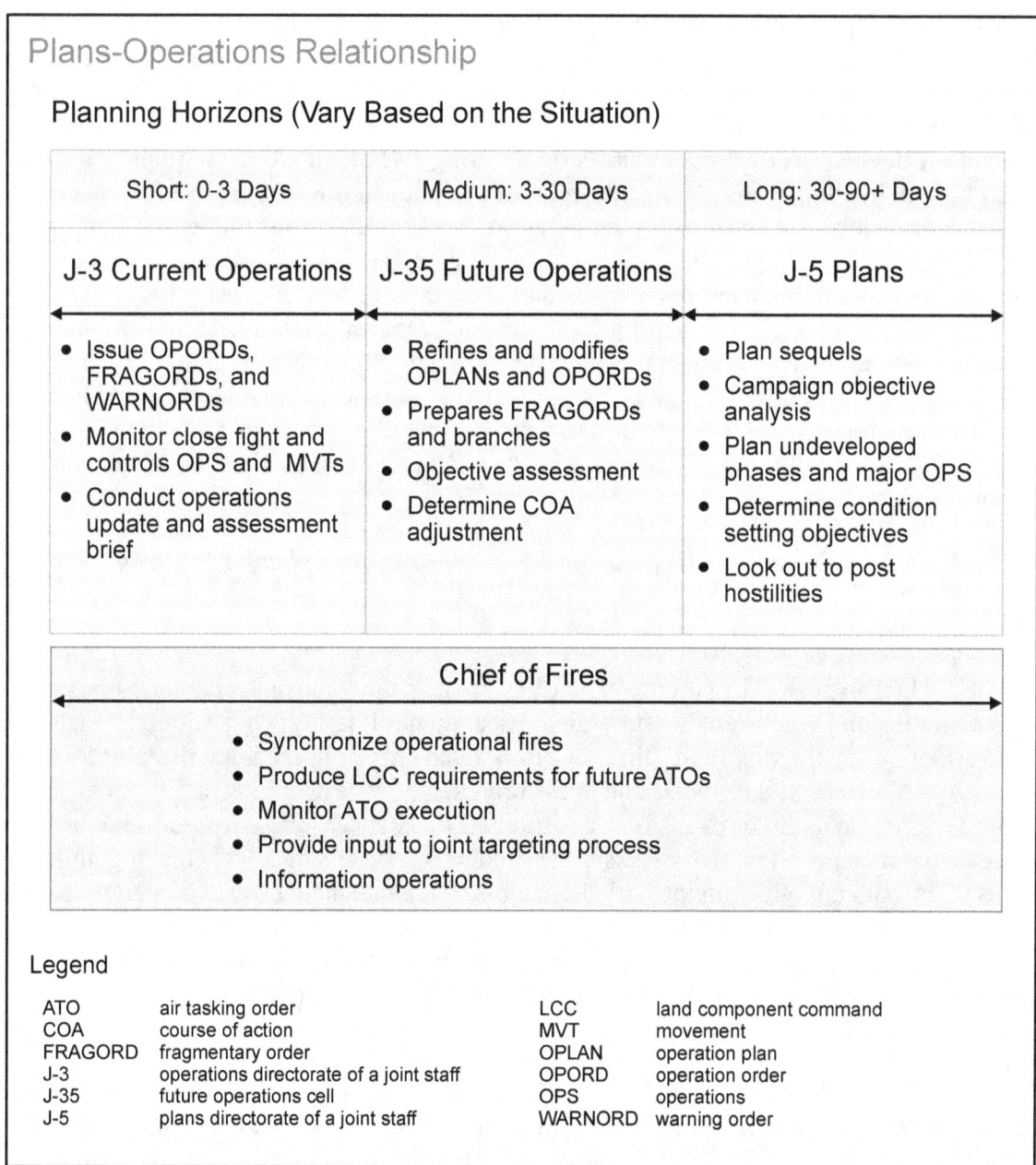

Figure III-2. Plans–Operations Relationship

protracted sequentially, but some activities from a phase may continue into subsequent phases or actually begin during a previous phase (see Figure III-3). The JFLCC adjusts the sub-phases to exploit opportunities presented by the adversary or operational situation or to react to unforeseen conditions.

(4) **Transitions.** Transitions between phases are designed to be distinct shifts in focus by the joint force, often accompanied by changes in command relationships. The need to move into another phase normally is identified by assessing that a set of objectives are achieved or that the enemy has acted in a manner that requires a major change in focus for the joint force and is therefore usually event driven, not time driven. Changing the focus of

Phasing Model

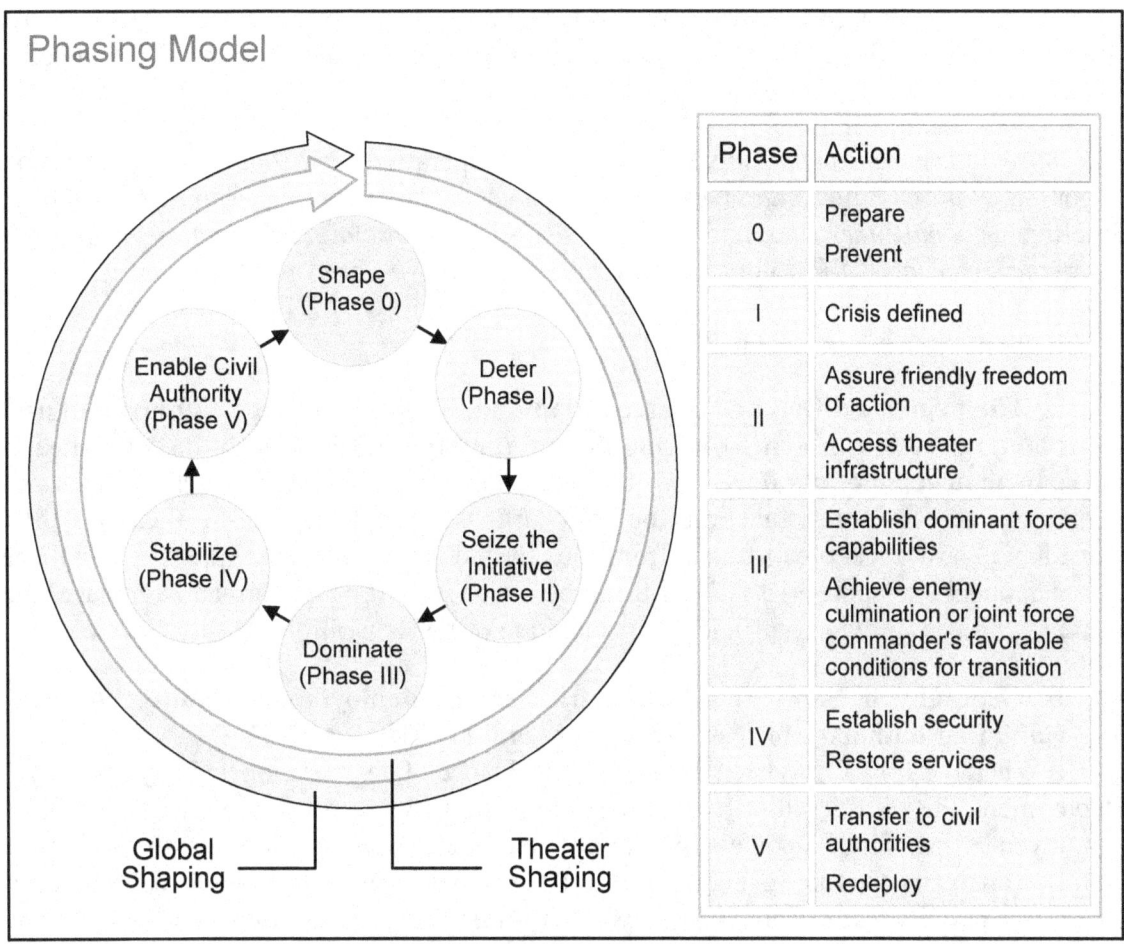

Phase	Action
0	Prepare Prevent
I	Crisis defined
II	Assure friendly freedom of action Access theater infrastructure
III	Establish dominant force capabilities Achieve enemy culmination or joint force commander's favorable conditions for transition
IV	Establish security Restore services
V	Transfer to civil authorities Redeploy

Figure III-3. Phasing Model

the operation takes time and may require changing priorities, command relationships, force allocation, or even the approach to the operation. An example is the shift of focus from sustained combat operations in the dominate phase to a preponderance of stability operations in the stabilize phase. Hostilities gradually lessen as the joint land force begins to reestablish order, commerce, and local government and deters adversaries from resuming hostile actions while the US and international community takes steps to establish or restore the conditions necessary to achieve their strategic objectives. Planning for the transition from phase IV (stabilize) to phase V (enable civil authority) demands an agile shift in joint land force skill sets, actions, organizational behaviors, and mental outlooks; and coordination with a wider range of other organizations—other USG departments and agencies, multinational partners, IGOs, and NGOs—to provide those capabilities necessary to address the mission-specific factors.

(5) **Phasing Model.** Although the JFC determines the number and actual phases used during a joint operation, use of the phases shape, deter, seize the initiative, dominate, stabilize, and enable civil authority shown in Figure III-3 provides a flexible model to arrange smaller, related operations. This model can be applied to various campaigns and operations. Operations and activities in the "shape" and "deter" phases normally are outlined in a theater campaign plan and those in the remaining phases are outlined in JSCP-directed

OPLANs. By design, OPLANs generally do not include security cooperation activities that are addressed elsewhere. JFLCCs generally use the phasing model in Figure III-3 to link the pertinent OPLAN and activities with that of the JFC.

For more information on phasing, see JP 3-0, Joint Operations, *and JP 5-0,* Joint Operation Planning. *For more information on intelligence support and planning, refer to JP 2-0,* Joint Intelligence, *and other JP 2-0-Series publications. For more information on logistic planning, refer to JP 4-0,* Joint Logistics, *and other JP 4-0-Series publications.*

4. **Operational Planning Considerations**

a. **The primary difference between planning for single-Service employment and joint land operations is synchronizing the unique capabilities and limitations of each force to achieve unity of effort.** This requires an understanding of these capabilities and limitations across all staff functions, but it is particularly important in the JPG. The JPG must have knowledgeable members from each Service in all functional areas. With these key personnel and appropriate LNOs from the major subordinate commands in place, the planning process provides sufficient consideration of the capabilities of each Service.

b. **Generally the Service component will perform deployment planning; however, the validating authority for Service component TPFDDs or RFFs/RFCs will be the JFC.** When the JFLCC has been designated in advance of an operation and any associated deployment, the JFLCC will influence the deployment process for those units that will be employed by the JFLCC upon completion of integration. In practical terms, this influence involves analyzing the force generation requirements to determine the required dates for each force or capability made available to the JFLCC. Further, priorities may be established by the JFLCC to aid the JFC in allocating limited lift or port capabilities in a way that best supports the JFLCC's CONOPS.

c. When conducted, the force deployment planning performed by the plans directorate of a joint staff (J-5) deployment cell must be in concert with the JPG's operational planning. The deployment planners require visibility on the capabilities and sequencing priorities associated with a COA or CONOPS to ensure they are transportable and the deployment requirements are relayed to the JFC. The JFLCC's planning staff must remember that the timing and sequencing priority may be affected by the JFC's overall concept of deployment.

5. **Joint Land Operations Plan**

a. **General. JFLCC joint land OPLANs, joint land operation plans in concept format (CONPLANs), and OPORDs convey how the land force helps accomplish the JFC's mission.** The plans developed by the JFLCC describe the intended conduct of joint land operations that support the achievement of JFC's objectives.

b. The OPORD describes the synchronization of specific tasks that result in an effective employment of joint/multinational land force capabilities for a major operation. The CONOPS, included in paragraph 3 ("Execution), also provides the concepts of movement and maneuver, fires, protection, intelligence operations, and IO. The concept of sustainment is included in paragraph 4, while the concept of C2 is in paragraph 5. All are included in the final OPLAN or order.

c. OPLANs, CONPLANs, and OPORDs are distributed internally to the land force for action and externally to the JFC for approval and Service and functional component commands for information. If OPLANs, CONPLANs, or OPORDs describe a branch or sequel to the current plan, they are distributed externally to the JFC for approval and to the Service and other functional component commanders for information.

d. Planning products are distributed simultaneously to all JFLCC subordinate commanders. This allows them to adequately evaluate the impact of future plans and operations from an operational perspective; however, the Service component commands must be concurrently involved in order to assess and plan for support to the JFLCC.

See Appendix C, "Joint Land Operation Plan and Order Development," for more information on a joint land OPLAN.

6. Operational Environment

a. **General.** Factors that must be considered when conducting joint land operations extend beyond the boundaries of the JFLCC's assigned operational area. **The operational environment is the composite of the conditions, circumstances, and influences that affect the employment of capabilities and bear on the decisions of the commander. It normally encompasses the physical areas and factors of the air, land, maritime, and space domains, as well as the information environment (which includes cyberspace). Included within these are the adversary, friendly, and neutral systems that are relevant to a specific joint land operation.** Understanding the operational environment helps commanders understand the results of various friendly, adversary, and neutral actions and how this impacts attaining the military end state (see Figure III-4).

b. **Physical Areas and Factors**

(1) **Physical Areas.** The pertinent physical areas in the operational environment include the assigned operational area and the associated areas of influence and interest described below. Designation of the areas of influence and interest help commanders and staffs order their thoughts during both planning and execution.

(a) The **AOR** is the geographical area associated with a combatant command within which a GCC has authority to plan and conduct operations.

(b) An **area of interest (AOI)** includes the area of influence, adjacent areas, and extends into hostile territory to the objectives of current or planned operations. An AOI focuses intelligence support for monitoring adversary or other activities pertinent to the operational area that may affect operations. The commander can describe the AOI graphically, but the resulting graphic does not represent a boundary or other control measure.

(c) An **AOI** is a geographic area wherein a commander is directly capable of influencing operations by maneuver or fire support systems normally under the commander's

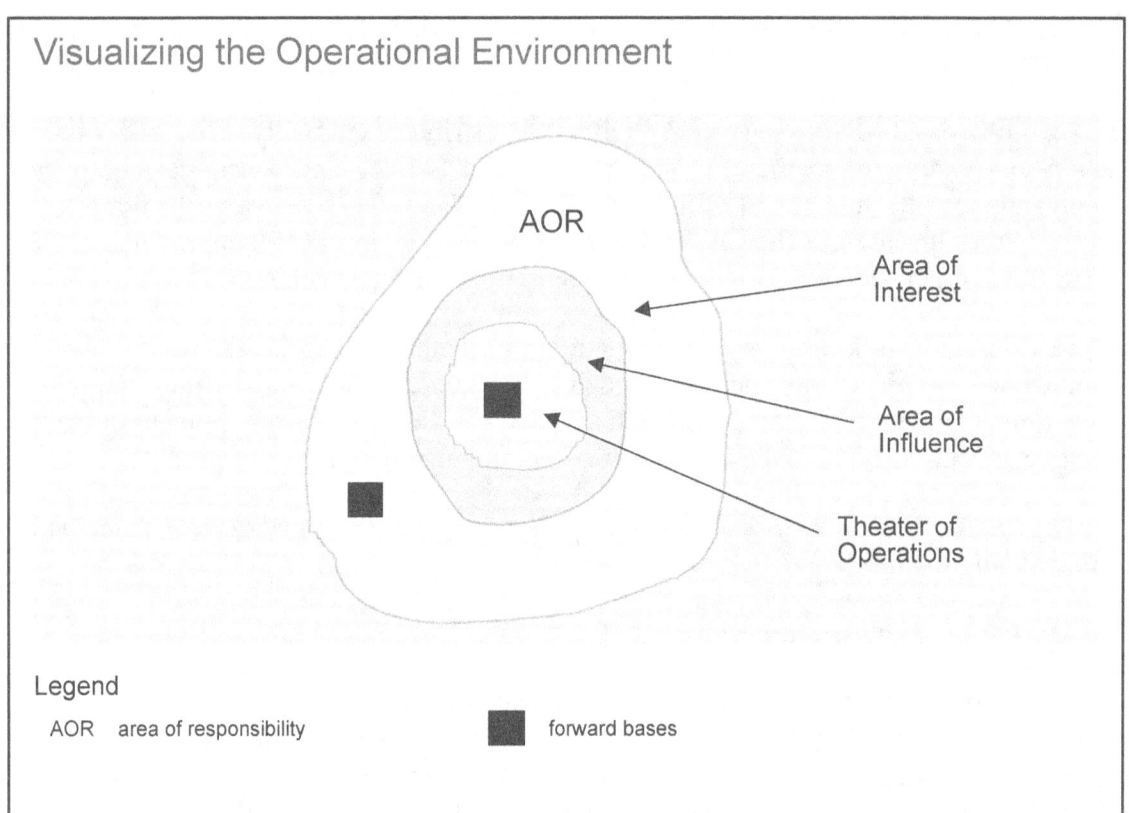

Figure III-4. Visualizing the Operational Environment

command or control. The area of influence normally surrounds and includes the assigned operational area. The extent of a subordinate command's area of influence is one factor the higher commander considers when defining the subordinate's operational area. Understanding the command's area of influence helps the commander and staff plan branches to the current operation that could require the force to employ capabilities outside the assigned operational area. The commander can describe the area of influence graphically, but the resulting graphic does not represent a boundary or other control measure for maneuver or fire support.

(d) A **theater of operations** is an operational area defined by the GCC for the conduct or support of specific military operations. Multiple theaters of operations normally will be geographically separate and focused on different missions. Theaters of operations are usually of significant size, allowing for operations in depth and over extended periods of time.

(2) **Physical Factors.** The JFLCC and staff must consider numerous physical factors associated with operations in the operational area. These factors include terrain (including urban settings), weather, topography, hydrology, EMS, and environmental conditions in the operational area; distances associated with the deployment to the operational area and employment of forces and other joint capabilities; the location of bases, ports, and other supporting infrastructure (such as key cyberspace nodes); and both friendly and adversary forces and other capabilities. Combinations of these factors greatly affect the operational design and sustainment of joint land operations.

c. **Information Environment.** The information environment is the aggregate of individuals, organizations, and systems that collect, process, disseminate, or act on information. For analytical purposes, the information environment consists of three interrelated dimensions which continuously interact with individuals, organizations, and systems. These dimensions are the physical, informational, and cognitive.

See JP 3-0, Joint Operations, *and JP 2-01.3,* Joint Intelligence Preparation of the Operational Environment, *for more information on the operational environment. See JP 3-13,* Information Operations, *for specific information on the information environment. See JP 3-12,* Cyberspace Operations, *for specific information on cyberspace.*

d. **Human and Cultural Factors.** The JFLCC and staff must consider numerous human and cultural factors associated with their operational environment. These factors include all aspects of social, cultural, religious, language, economics, and politics as they affect friendly, neutral, and adversary capabilities. Each of these human and cultural factors is essential to understanding the root causes of conflicts, developing appropriate approaches, and anticipating second-order effects as these can greatly affect the operational design and conduct of joint land operations.

7. Conventional and Special Operations Force Integration

a. The JTF C2 organization should consider the unique SOF organizational structures, along with their capabilities and limitations in the same manner as those of the different Service land forces. The unique attributes of all land forces and their integration must be considered throughout planning and execution. To maximize efficiency, Services and USSOCOM rely on each other for various functions during operations.

b. Conventional forces and SOF require coordination and liaison at all levels of the joint force to ensure that C2 is fully integrated. The focal point for integration of SOF activities and conventional joint land operations is the special operations C2 element, which collocates with the supported or supporting command element of the joint force land component command. In addition, exchange of liaison personnel at various commands, organizations, or lower tactical levels may be required for improved communication.

c. The C2 elements of the joint force land component command operate in concert to execute the JFLCC's assigned missions. This requires organizations, systems, and equipment within conventional forces and SOF to be interoperable in order to effectively facilitate control of forces. The simplest and most streamlined C2 arrangement can be thwarted by the absence of interoperability among the components' forces and systems.

For additional information on SOF, refer to JP 3-05, Special Operations. *For information on conventional forces and SOF integration, see Army Tactical Publication 6-03.05/MCWP 3-36.1/Navy Tactics, Techniques, and Procedures (NTTP) 3-05.19/Air Force Tactics, Techniques, and Procedures (AFTTP) 3-2.73/USSOCOM Publication 3-33, v-3,* Multi-Service Tactics, Techniques, and Procedures for Conventional Forces and Special Operations Forces Synchronization.

SECTION B. ASSESSMENT

8. General

a. **Assessment is a process that measures progress** of the joint force toward mission accomplishment. **Commanders continuously assess** the operational environment and the progress of operations and compare them to their vision and intent. Commanders adjust operations based on their assessment to ensure military objectives are met and the military end state is attained. **The assessment process is continuous and directly tied to the commander's decisions** throughout planning, preparation, and execution of operations. Staffs help the commander by monitoring the numerous aspects that can influence the outcome of operations and provide the commander timely information needed for decisions. **The CCIR process is linked to the assessment process** by the commander's need for timely information and recommendations to make decisions. The assessment process helps staffs by identifying key aspects of the operation that the commander is interested in closely monitoring and where the commander wants to make decisions. Examples of commander's critical decisions include when to transition to another phase of an operation, what the priority of effort should be, or how to adjust command relationships between component commanders.

b. The assessment process begins during mission analysis when the commander and staff consider what to measure and how to measure it **to determine progress toward accomplishing a task, creating an effect, or achieving an objective.** During planning and preparation for an operation, for example, the staff assesses the joint force's ability to execute the plan based on available resources and changing conditions in the operational environment. However, **the discussion in this section focuses on assessment for the purpose of determining the progress of the joint force toward mission accomplishment.**

c. Commanders and their staffs **determine relevant assessment actions and measures during planning.** They consider assessment measures as early as mission analysis and include assessment measures and related guidance in commander and staff estimates. They use assessment considerations to help guide operational design because these considerations can affect the sequence and type of actions along lines of operation. During execution, they continually monitor progress toward accomplishing tasks, creating effects, and achieving objectives. Assessment actions and measures help commanders adjust operations and resources as required, determine when to execute branches and sequels, and make other critical decisions to ensure current and future operations remain aligned with the mission and military end state. Normally, the JFLCC chief of staff, assisted by the J-3 and the J-2, is responsible for coordinating assessment activities. The chief of staff is normally also assisted by an assessment special staff section which may include personnel to do operations research and systems analysis (ORSA), sociocultural experts, and others. For subordinate commanders' staffs, this may be accomplished by equivalent elements within Service components. The chief of staff normally facilitates the assessment process and determination of CCIRs by incorporating them into the headquarters' battle rhythm. Various elements of the JFC's staff use assessment results to adjust both current operations and future planning.

d. Friendly, adversary, and neutral diplomatic, informational, and economic actions applied in the operational environment can impact military actions and objectives. When relevant to the mission, the commander also must plan for using assessment to evaluate the results of these actions. This typically requires collaboration with other USG departments and agencies and multinational partners—preferably within a common, accepted process—in the interest of unified action. Many of these organizations may be outside the JFLCC's authority. Accordingly, the JFLCC should grant some organizations authority for direct coordination with key outside organizations—such as interagency elements from DOS, DHS, and national intelligence agencies; intelligence sources in other nations; and other components—to the extent necessary to ensure timely and accurate assessments.

9. Levels of Operations and Assessment

Assessment occurs at all levels of military operations. Even in operations that do not include combat, assessment of progress is just as important and can be more complex than traditional combat assessment. As a general rule, the level at which a specific operation, task, or action is directed should be the level at which such activity is assessed. Assessment at the operational and strategic levels typically is broader than at the tactical level (e.g., combat assessment) and uses MOEs that support strategic and operational mission accomplishment. Continuous assessment helps the JFLCC determine if the joint land force is doing the right things to achieve its objectives. Tactical-level assessment typically uses measures of performance to evaluate task accomplishment. The results of tactical tasks are often physical in nature, but also can reflect the impact on specific functions and systems. Combat assessment is an example of a tactical level assessment and is a term that can encompass many tactical-level assessment actions. Combat assessment is composed of three major components: battle damage assessment, munitions effectiveness assessment, and future targeting and reattack recommendations.

See JP 5-0, Joint Operation Planning, *and JP 3-60,* Joint Targeting, *for more information on assessment.*

Intentionally Blank

CHAPTER IV
OPERATIONS

> "…no plan of operation can extend with any prospect of certainty, beyond the first clash with the hostile main force. Only a layman can pretend to trace throughout the course of a campaign the prosecution of a rigid plan, arranged beforehand in all its details and adhered to the last."
>
> **Helmuth Graf von Moltke (The Elder), 1800-1891**

SECTION A. FORMS OF OPERATIONS

1. General

a. JFCs strive to apply the many dimensions of military power to address both traditional warfare and irregular warfare (IW) simultaneously across the depth, breadth, and height of the operational area. Consequently, JFCs normally achieve concentration in some operations or in specific functions and require economy of force in others. All joint OPLANs must feature an appropriate combination and balance between offensive and defensive operations and stability operations in all phases. Planning for stability operations should begin when joint operation planning is initiated. Planning for the transition from sustained land combat operations to the termination of joint operations and then a complete handover to civil authority and redeployment must commence during plan development and be ongoing during all phases of a joint campaign or major operation. An isolated focus on planning offensive and defensive operations in the dominate phase may threaten full development of basic and supporting plans for the stabilize and enable civil authority phases and ultimately joint operation momentum. Even while sustained land operations are ongoing, there will be a need to establish or restore security and provide humanitarian relief as succeeding areas are occupied or bypassed. While joint land operations conducted outside the US and its territories simultaneously combine three elements—offense, defense, and stability; joint land operations within the US primary focus on HD and DSCA operations.

b. Excessive civilian casualties can severely undermine joint land operations and are increasingly transparent to external actors. Joint land forces are expected to uphold the highest legal standards. These standards gain extra scrutiny in an environment where the adversary will make false accusations and seek to exploit mistakes. Further, the local population's support is often critical to mission success, and civilian casualties can place such support in jeopardy. Minimizing and addressing civilian casualty incidents frequently supports strategic imperatives and is also at the heart of the profession of arms. Civilian casualty mitigation includes predeployment training and post-incident investigation and response. Leadership is vital for effective civilian casualty mitigation procedures. Commanders should ensure that joint land forces routinely incorporate civilian casualty mitigation when planning and conducting land operations ranging from collateral damage estimation during joint targeting, to use of nonlethal capabilities, to safety during road movements. Additionally, a commander may establish a civilian casualty tracking cell to systematically monitor a civilian casualty mitigation cycle: prepare, plan, employ, assess, respond, and learn. Commanders should be aware that civilian casualties can be mitigated through efforts that begin long before a particular incident—indeed, long before deployment—and the impacts of civilian casualties continue after the incident has occurred.

See Army Tactics, Techniques, and Procedures (ATTP) 3-37.31, Civilian Casualty Mitigation, *for detailed information.*

2. Offensive Operations

a. Major operations and campaigns, whether or not they involve large-scale ground combat, normally will include some level of both **offense and defense.** Although defense may be the stronger force posture, the offense is normally decisive in combat. Further, protection includes certain defensive measures that are required throughout each joint operation or campaign phase. The relationship between offense and defense, then, is a complementary one.

b. Offensive land operations are combat operations conducted to defeat and destroy enemy land forces and seize terrain, resources, and population centers. Offensive land operations impose the commander's will on the enemy. Against a capable, adaptive enemy, the offense is the most direct and sure means to seize, retain, and exploit the initiative to achieve decisive results. Executing offensive land operations compels the enemy to react, creating or revealing weakness that the entire attacking joint force can exploit. Successful ground offensive operations place tremendous pressure on defenders, creating a cycle of deterioration that can lead to their disintegration.

c. At the operational and strategic level of war, the Armed Forces of the United States must be capable of deploying and fighting to gain access to geographic areas controlled by hostile forces. **Forcible entry** is the seizing and holding of a military **lodgment** in the face of armed opposition. **Forcible entry** operations are normally joint in nature and range in scope from an operation planned as an initial phase of a campaign or major operation to a **coup de main** in which the decisive results are accomplished in one swift stroke. The Armed Forces of the United States maintain three primary forcible entry capabilities or options. These are amphibious assault, airborne assault, and air assault. Local air and/or maritime superiority are essential for the duration of the forcible entry operation. JFCs typically seek to attain more comprehensive control of the potential operating environment, permitting as many such options as possible to frustrate opposing defense planning. JFCs may select one entry capability or a combination based upon analysis of the situation and the threat. JFLCCs may be tasked by the JFC to perform the detailed planning for a forcible entry operation.

For more specifics, see JP 3-18, Joint Forcible Entry Operations.

d. Countering WMD operations designed to control adversary WMD and to immediately reduce the threat of use, proliferation, or loss may be a component part of forcible entry operations. When an adversary possesses WMD or elements of a WMD program, land operations may be the primary mechanism by which the threat of WMD is reduced or eliminated. A JTF for WMD elimination is a functional JTF controlled by the JFC and will normally support the JFLCC. The Standing Joint Force Headquarters for

Elimination of Weapons of Mass Destruction is a standing joint element that plans and trains for C2 of elimination operations in support of geographic combatant commands, and on order, deploys to enable an existing headquarters or to provide the core of a JTF headquarters that executes elimination operations.

e. Stability operations cannot occur if significant enemy forces directly threaten or attack the local populace. Offensive land control operations destroy or isolate the enemy so stability operations can proceed by denying enemy forces the opportunity to seize additional terrain, moving them out of population centers of gravity (COGs), and forcing enemy forces to defend their bases.

3. Defensive Operations

a. Defensive operations are combat operations conducted to defeat an enemy attack, gain time, economize forces, and develop conditions favorable for offensive or stability operations. Defense alone is normally not a decisive action. However, defensive land operations enable JFLCCs to conduct or prepare for decisive offensive or stability operations. Defensive land control operations retain terrain, guard populations, and protect critical capabilities against enemy attacks and are used to gain time and economize forces so offensive tasks can be executed elsewhere.

b. Joint land forces protect vital military and civilian areas in joint operational areas for the JFC that are important to the overall operational success and provide indirect support to all joint operations. Joint land forces defend joint lodgments and bases ensuring freedom of action to joint air, maritime, and SOF. This defense may consist of land based AMD units, chemical, biological, and radiological warning and decontamination units, as well as ground forces physically protecting facilities or terrain using lethal and nonlethal weapons systems.

c. Defense of the local populace, infrastructure, and vital assets supports stability operations and allows joint land forces to receive greater support from the HN. This protection is vital to joint COIN operations where some facilities have significant economic and political value to the local population.

4. Stability Operations

a. Stability operations encompass various military missions, tasks, and activities conducted outside the US in coordination with other instruments of national power to maintain or reestablish a safe and secure environment, provide essential governmental services, emergency infrastructure reconstruction, and humanitarian relief. Joint land forces assume that role before, during, and after conducting land operations, across the range of operations. In doing so, the efforts of military forces appropriately focus in support of the other instruments of national and international power. Stability operations will not only include stability tasks, but will often have elements of offense and defense. For land forces, these efforts are fundamental to the conduct of joint operations.

b. **Stability operations** can be conducted in support of an HN or interim government or as part of an occupation when no government exists. Stability operations must maintain the initiative by pursuing objectives that resolve the causes of instability. Stability operations cannot succeed if they only react to enemy initiatives. Stability operations involve both coercive and constructive military actions. Joint land force stability operations are often conducted within the broader context of USG reconstruction and stabilization efforts. Joint land forces support these broader efforts by leveraging the coercive and constructive capabilities of the force to establish a safe and secure environment; facilitate reconciliation among local or regional adversaries; establish or restore political, legal, social, and economic institutions; and help transition responsibility to a legitimate civil authority operating under the rule of law. This transition is fundamental to the shift in focus toward long-term developmental activities where joint land forces support broader efforts in pursuit of national and international objectives. Success in these endeavors typically requires a long-term commitment by IGOs and NGOs and is ultimately determined by the support and participation of the HN population.

c. Joint land forces establish conditions that enable the efforts of the other instruments of national and international power through unified action. By providing the requisite security and control to stabilize an operational area, those efforts build a foundation for transitioning to civilian control and eventually to the HN. Stability operations are usually conducted to support an HN government or a transitional civil or military authority when no legitimate, functioning HN government exists. Generally, joint land forces establish or restore basic civil functions and protect them until a civil authority or the HN is capable of providing these services for the local populace. They perform specific functions as part of a broader response effort, supporting the complementary activities of other agencies, organizations, and the private sector. When the HN or other agency cannot fulfill its role, joint land forces may be called upon to significantly increase their role, including providing the basic civil functions of government.

d. By nature, stability operations are typically lengthy endeavors. All tasks must be performed with a focus toward maintaining the delicate balance between long-term success and short-term gains. Ultimately, stability operations do not necessarily aim to reduce the military presence quickly but to achieve broader national policy goals that extend beyond the objectives of joint military operations. The more effective those military efforts are at setting conditions that facilitate the efforts of the other instruments of national power, the more likely it is that the long-term commitment of substantial joint land forces will not be required. Nonlethal capabilities provide ground forces an escalation of force capability to determine intent during operations and assist in reducing civilian casualties, helping to gain the trust of the population.

e. To that end, joint land forces have to operate with other joint forces and the other instruments of national power to forge unity of effort through a whole-of-government approach. This approach accounts for a wider range of considerations beyond those of the military instrument, ensuring that planning accounts for broader national policy goals and interests. For the JFLCC and staff, this may mean planning and executing joint land operations within an environment of political ambiguity. As a result, the potentially slow development process of government reconstruction and stabilization policy may frustrate flexible military plans that adapt to the lethal dynamics of land combat operations. Thus, integrating the planning efforts of all the agencies and organizations involved in a stability operation is essential to long-term peace and stability.

f. **Stability Operations Activities, Tasks, and Functions.** The activities, tasks, and functions that make up stability operations fall into three broad categories and five functions.

(1) Initial response activities are tasks executed to stabilize the operational environment in an area of crisis, for instance during or immediately following a conflict or a natural disaster. As land control operations clear areas of hostile forces, initial response activities by joint land forces aim to provide a safe, secure environment and attend to the immediate humanitarian needs of the indigenous population. They support efforts to reduce the level of violence or human suffering while creating conditions that enable other organizations to participate safely in ongoing efforts.

(2) Transformational activities are a broad range of security, reconstruction, and capacity building efforts. These activities require the absence of major threats to friendly forces and the populace and aim to build HN capacity across multiple sectors. These activities establish conditions that facilitate unified action to rebuild the HN and its supporting institutions.

(3) Activities that foster sustainability encompass long-term efforts that capitalize on capacity building and reconstruction activities to establish conditions that enable sustainable development. Properly focused, effectively executed stability tasks by a land component may prevent population centers from degenerating into civil unrest and becoming recruiting areas for opposition movements or insurgencies.

(4) Stability operations functions are linked to the DOS reconstruction and stabilization sectors. Normally joint land forces act in support of HN and other civilian agencies. However, when the HN cannot provide basic government functions, joint land forces may be required to do so directly. The DOD stability operations functions are security, governance and participation, humanitarian assistance, economic stabilization and infrastructure, and rule of law.

For further details on stability operations, see JP 3-07, Stability Operations.

g. To attain the national strategic end state and conclude the operation/campaign successfully, JFLCCs must integrate and synchronize stability operations with other joint land operations (offense and defense) within each major operation or campaign phase. Stability operations support USG plans for stability and reconstruction efforts and likely will be conducted in coordination with, and in support of, HN authorities, other USG departments and agencies, IGOs, and/or NGOs, and the private sector.

5. Defense Support of Civil Authorities

a. Military operations inside the US and its territories, though limited in many respects, are conducted to accomplish two missions: HD and DSCA. A JFLCC is often used to provide C2 for land operations for DSCA.

b. DSCA consists of DOD support to US civil authorities for domestic emergencies, both man-made and natural, and for designated law enforcement and other activities, such as national special security events. This includes DOD forces when directed by the President or

---

HURRICANE SANDY, OCTOBER 2012

US Army North (USARNORTH)/US Northern Command Joint Force Land Component Commander (JFLCC) coordinated defense support of civil authorities for Hurricane Sandy by conducting the following actions:

1. Estimated impact of the storm.

2. Pre-positioned USARNORTH assessment team.

3. Identified Title 10, United States Code, troop requirements based on potential mission assignments in coordination with the Federal Emergency Management Agency.

4. Determined federal command and control (C2) structure; issued Fragmentary Order 42; activated dual status joint task forces.

5. Deployed theater opening elements (movement control, personnel reception, base support); alerted/deployed other federal forces to joint operations area (JOA).

6. Deployed Commanding General and JFLCC Coordination Element (JCE) personnel.

7. JCE fully operational providing: operational C2 over all federal and state dual-status forces in JOA; theater logistics support; operational general support and direct support logistics; strategic mobility coordination; execution of operational missions; situational assessment; and reporting.

8. Redeployed JCE following departure of all federal forces and clearing bases; reporting shifted back to USARNORTH main command post.

Various Sources

SecDef. Federal agencies or state governors request DOD capabilities to support their emergency response efforts by using the federal request for assistance (RFA) process (National Guard forces employed under state active duty or Title 32, USC status are under the C2 of the governor of their state and are not part of federal military response efforts.) Dual-status commanders (with both federal and state authorities) provide useful options for command of JTFs established in response to an emergency or major disaster within the US. For DSCA operations, DOD supports but does not supplant civil authorities. DOD resources are normally used only when state and local resources are overwhelmed and/or non-DOD resources of the USG are insufficient or unable to meet the requirements of local and state civil authorities.

c. It is important to note that not all DSCA is provided via the RFA process, and can include counterdrug activities, intelligence or investigative support, or other support to civilian law enforcement in accordance with specific DOD policies and US law.

For more information on DSCA, refer to JP 3-28, Defense Support of Civil Authorities.

---

6. Types of Military Operations

The US employs its military capabilities at home and abroad in support of its national security goals in a variety of operations. Some operations conducted by a JFLCC may involve only steady-state, routine, recurring military activities that do not relate directly to either traditional war or IW. Other operations, such as COIN, support to insurgency, and combating terrorism, primarily involve IW. Operations such as nation assistance, foreign internal defense, peace operations, FHA, combating terrorism, counterdrug operations, show of force operations, and arms control are applied to meet military engagement, security cooperation, and deterrence objectives. Major operations and campaigns are typically characterized by large-scale combat operations associated with traditional war. All of these circumstances—each potentially with different root causes and objectives—can exist concurrently within a single operational area and may require consideration by a JFLCC.

See JP 3-0, Joint Operations, *for more detail on types of military operations.*

SECTION B. JOINT FUNCTIONS

7. General

a. In any joint land operation, the JFLCC and staff plan, direct, and coordinate a number of **joint functions** that are critical to the successful execution of joint land operations. **Joint functions are related capabilities and activities grouped together to help JFCs integrate, synchronize, and direct joint operations.** Functions that are common to joint operations at all levels of war fall into **six basic groups—C2, intelligence, fires, movement and maneuver, protection, and sustainment.** Some functions, such as C2 and intelligence, apply to all operations. Others, such as fires, apply as required by the mission.

b. A number of subordinate tasks, missions, and related capabilities help define each function. Some tasks, missions, and capabilities could apply to more than one joint function. For example, IRCs are applied across the joint functions and independently.

c. The JFLCC can choose from a wide variety of joint and Service capabilities and combine them in various ways to perform joint functions and accomplish the mission. The joint land OPLAN/OPORD describes the way joint land forces and assets are used together to perform joint functions and tasks. However, forces and assets are not characterized by the functions for which the JFLCC is employing them. A single force or asset can perform multiple functions simultaneously or sequentially while executing a single task. This section discusses the joint functions, related tasks, and key considerations as applicable to joint land operations. The JFLCC and staff must also monitor and may coordinate and synchronize the **support functions** (e.g., logistics, personnel support) that impact joint land operations.

For a more detailed discussion of joint functions, see JP 3-0, Joint Operations, *and CJCSM 3500.04,* Universal Joint Task Manual.

8. Command and Control

a. **General.** **C2** encompasses the exercise of authority and direction by a properly designated commander over assigned and attached forces in the accomplishment of the mission. The C2 function encompasses a number of tasks that are detailed in JP 3-0, *Joint Operations.*

b. The ability of the JFLCC or other commander tasked to conduct land operations is the result of leadership and the ability to control forces and functions in order to execute the intent. C2 is supported by an intelligence, surveillance, and reconnaissance (ISR) infrastructure and reliable and secure communications and computer systems. These systems process and integrate data and information and pass it to where it is needed and display it in a useable format in time to be acted upon. This combination of C2 and the tools for its implementation is fundamental to the conduct of modern military operations. The nature of the operational area accentuates the challenges to the JFLCC and offers significant hindrances to effective C2. The integration of intelligence data and assessments, shared at the collateral level, with sensor and tactical network data available in the joint operations center is a key element in maintaining an accurate picture of land operations.

c. Understanding and shaping the operational area is extremely challenging. The key to understanding the operational environment at all levels is the ability to rapidly collect and disseminate information. Critical to shaping this operational environment is the ability to convert information into knowledge that can be used to make and then implement command decisions. Since any joint land operation contains a great deal of uncertainty, and since knowledge is a perishable asset, then speed and precision are necessary to convert the right information into knowledge as expediently as possible.

d. **C2 Considerations in Land Operations**

(1) The complex physical environment of the operational area may restrict the performance of some technologies supporting C2, including line of sight communications and overhead surveillance. Mountains and jungles can present barriers to communication systems. Subterranean and interior spaces also make timely understanding of the urban operational environment even more difficult.

(2) The presence of civilians further complicates land C2. The JFLCC must always consider the effects of operations on civilians, and their presence in large numbers will require great attention to areas such as CMO, interagency support, and the public affairs officer (PAO). Existing infrastructure such as transportation and communication systems can both facilitate and hinder C2. Service infrastructure such as police, fire, and medical services may offer control and information opportunities, but its absence contributes to joint force responsibilities.

(3) As joint land operations tend to become decentralized, mission command becomes the preferred method of C2. Mission command is the conduct of military operations through decentralized execution based upon mission-type orders. It empowers individuals to exercise judgment in how they carry out their assigned tasks and it exploits the

human element in joint operations emphasizing trust, force of will, initiative, judgment, and creativity. Successful mission command demands that subordinate leaders at all echelons exercise disciplined initiative, acting aggressively and independently to accomplish the mission. Orders are focused on the purpose of the operation rather than the details of how to perform assigned tasks. Essential to mission command is the thorough knowledge and understanding of the commander's intent at every level of command and a command climate of mutual trust and understanding. Under mission command, commanders issue mission-type orders, use implicit communications, delegate most decisions to subordinates wherever possible and minimize detailed control. When joint land operations are decentralized and reliant on mission command, coordination of joint operations must be planned with consideration of the procedures, measures, and resources (including time) required to implement those plans. In such conditions the JFLCC and staff must anticipate requirements to identify demands for joint support, prioritize among operations or force elements, and communicate extensively with other affected components. In addition, the JFLCC and staff must determine what procedures must remain under centralized control (i.e., ROE, communications, integrated AMD, joint fires) to ensure standardization across the JFLCC's AO.

(4) In joint land operations, the **CCIR** categories of priority intelligence requirements and friendly force information requirements must also include pertinent information concerning the land environment. Friendly information may include items such as anticipated political actions by an HN, the ability of the HN to support civilians, or the presence of sufficient precision munitions in the joint force. Although the adversary may consist of a traditional armed force, priority intelligence requirements on criminal elements, guerrillas, terrorists, and tribal or political factions may be necessary. Environmental information requirements may include elements of the environment, such as the behavior and needs of civilians or the presence or likelihood of disease or hunger.

(5) In joint land operations, it is imperative that an AO be established that includes sufficient area for the JFLCC to achieve the objectives. The AOI should include any area from which influence can be exerted on the land AO. Other operational areas may be designated outside or inside the JOA. Airspace coordinating measures (ACMs), FSCMs, boundaries, and movement control measures must be carefully considered and delineated to allow maximum flexibility on the part of subordinate land commanders and to prevent friendly fire incidents.

(6) Information-sharing relationships and protocols between the JFLCC, local and national authorities, the country team, USG departments and agencies, IGOs, and NGOs must be established at the earliest stages of planning.

e. **Communications.** The nature of joint land operations present certain challenges to C2 and particularly to communications. Communications challenges are influenced by decentralization, the three dimensional nature of the operational area, urban terrain, or complex environmental hindrances to radio communications, and often the existence of a local communications infrastructure.

(1) Ground operations are inherently decentralized and the forces involved require the ability to communicate quickly outside the normal communication patterns. Because of the complexity of the environment, situational awareness, a COP, and visualization is very difficult. The communications system architecture should support the entire land area—vertical and horizontal, surface and subterranean, airspace, and littoral. In addition, the JFLCC may need to provide support to, or liaison with, embassy personnel, partner nations, local government personnel, and other components of the joint force.

(2) **Joint network operations (NETOPS) are the means by which communications are established and maintained throughout the DODIN. Commander, United States Strategic Command (CDRUSSTRATCOM)** is the supported commander for global CO to secure, operate, and defend DODIN. CDRUSSTRATCOM cyberspace efforts are coordinated by US Cyber Command who in turn coordinates with the GCC at the GCC's joint cyberspace center. As the JFLCC's single control agency for the management and operational direction of the joint communications network, the joint network operations control center **(JNCC) must be knowledgeable concerning the requirements of communications in the land environment, especially in the specific operational area.** The JNCC should be aware of the capabilities present in the urban area, their potential use, and any problems associated with that use. Vital to communications management is the need to support planning and execution to include information exchange requirements, radio frequency spectrum allocation, communications equipment dispersion, and assessment of communications effectiveness.

See CJCSM 6715.01, Joint Operational Employment of Virtual Collaboration, *and JP 6-0,* Joint Communications System, *for a full discussion of communications considerations.*

f. **Space Capabilities for C2**

(1) Space systems may be employed to monitor land areas before friendly forces are established. If the individual designated to be the JFLCC is also designated to be the SCA, he will normally designate a senior space officer who facilitates coordination, integration, and staffing activities for space operations on a daily basis.

(2) Space systems provide **ISR; missile tracking; launch detection; environmental monitoring; satellite communications; position, navigation, and timing; and navigation warfare.** Considering the difficulties in communications in and around land areas, space systems offers the JFLCC the ability to exchange information inside the operational area, between elements of the joint force, and also facilitates intertheater and intratheater communications. Space systems may form a critical link in the C2 architecture that rapidly passes data and information. This can enable taskings and warnings to forces, as well as critical situational awareness and location information. Space systems face simultaneous demands from many users and require prioritization.

(3) The space-based **Global Positioning System (GPS)** provides a critical capability during joint land operations. GPS can provide position, location, and velocity for weapon accuracy, ingress and egress, location, silent rendezvous coordination, and improved personnel situational awareness. The ability of space systems to provide real time terrain

information that, enhanced by imagery data, can be used by all components of the joint force is especially crucial to the success of ground forces.

See JP 3-14, Space Operations, *for a full discussion of space operations.*

g. **Risk Management.** Risk management is a function of command and is based on the amount of risk a higher authority is willing to accept. Risk management assists commanders in conserving lives and resources and avoiding or mitigating unnecessary risk, making an informed decision to execute a mission, identifying feasible and effective control measures where specific standards do not exist, and providing reasonable alternatives for mission accomplishment.

(1) High-tempo land operations may increase the risk of injury and death due to mishaps.

(2) JFLCCs and their staffs develop or institute a risk management process tailored to their particular mission or operational area. Joint land operations in general also tend to produce a significant number of injuries due to the nature of urban and complex terrain—falls from buildings or mountains, vehicular accident injuries, injuries caused by bodies of water or by weather extremes. Cities pose their own safety hazards even in the absence of an enemy. Urban hazards cause injuries not normally seen in large numbers in other types of terrain. Command interest, discipline, risk mitigation measures, and training lessen those risks. The JFLCC reduces the chance of mishap by conducting risk assessments, assigning a safety officer and staff, implementing a safety program, and seeking advice from local personnel. Safety considerations could include the geospatial and weather data, local road conditions and driving habits, uncharted or uncleared mine fields, and special equipment hazards.

h. **CMO.** CMO are the activities of a commander that establish collaborative relationships among military forces, governmental and nongovernmental, and civilian organizations and authorities, and the civilian populace in a permissive, uncertain, or hostile operational area in order to facilitate military operations nested in support of the overall US objectives. CMO may include performance by military forces of activities and functions normally the responsibility of the local, regional, or national government. These activities may occur throughout the range of military operations, and are the responsibility of the commander. CMO may also occur, if directed, in the absence of other military operations. A JFLCC will normally be supported by a US Army CA command or brigade. The command or brigade also has the ability to form the nucleus of a joint CMO TF, if directed. JFCs ensure CA and the execution of civil affairs operations (CAO) are integrated into the plan. CAO are a vital component of CMO and require planning and synchronization within the land component command, HN government, military and security forces, other USG departments and agencies, IGO, NGO, indigenous populations and institutions (IPI) to ensure maximum effectiveness.

For additional guidance on CMO, refer to JP 3-57, Civil-Military Operations, *and FM 3-57,* Civil Affairs Operations.

i. **PA.** The JFLCC must plan, conduct, and assess PA activities. PA is a core joint force function and is a critical component of the operational planning and risk assessment processes. PA informs key audiences and counters adversary propaganda and disinformation by providing a continuous flow of credible, reliable, timely, and accurate information to military members, their families, the media, and the public. The PAO anticipates and advises JFLCCs on the possible impact of military operations and activities within the public information realm and works with the JFLCC and staff to mitigate or address potentially compromising coverage. Because PA and IO plan and conduct public information activities, the JFLCC must ensure appropriate coordination to maximize effectiveness and ensure success.

For additional information on PA support, see JP 3-61, Public Affairs.

9. Intelligence

a. **The JFLCC defines intelligence responsibilities for the land component, prioritizes intelligence requirements of subordinate land forces, and provides representation for the land component and its subordinates.** The staff incorporates and synchronizes intelligence efforts, including human intelligence and CI efforts with the JFC's staff. The JFLCC is the JFC's focal point for adversary ground forces intelligence, target development, and combat assessment. The JFLCC states operational requirements and provides continuous feedback to ensure optimum ISR support to operations. The first step for filling JFLCC intelligence gaps should be to request augmentation from theater and/or national assets. Asset support is essential:

(1) To support the commander.

(2) To identify, define, and nominate targets.

(3) To support operational planning and execution.

(4) To avoid surprise and increase understanding of the operational area.

(5) To assist friendly deception efforts.

(6) To evaluate the results of operations.

(7) To assess opponent's vulnerability.

(8) To coordinate the use of the electronic frequency spectrum for electronic attack and communications.

(9) For warning of adversary WMD use, collecting information about WMD program and network elements for targeting and control requirements, and to facilitate actions to conduct operations in chemical, biological, radiological, and nuclear (CBRN) environments.

b. **Offices, Centers, and Teams.** While not all of the offices, centers, or teams available may be required, a JFLCC may request a national intelligence support team, joint interrogation and debriefing center, or joint document exploitation center.

See JP 2-0, Joint Intelligence, *JP 2-01,* Joint and National Intelligence Support to Military Operations, *and JP 2-01.3,* Joint Intelligence Preparation of the Operational Environment, *for more information.*

10. **Fires**

a. **General. The JFLCC plans, coordinates, synchronizes, and executes all joint fires to create lethal or nonlethal effects in order to set the conditions for success in their AOs. Joint fires** are delivered during the employment of forces from two or more components in coordinated action to produce desired effects in support of a common objective. **The JFLCC's focus is on shaping those opponent formations, functions, facilities, and operations that could impact on the JFLCC's AO.** The JFLCC has four primary goals associated with these operations.

(1) Facilitating both operational and tactical maneuver by suppressing the adversary's long range systems, disrupting the adversary's operational maneuver and tempo, and creating exploitable gaps in adversary positions.

(2) Isolating the operational area by interdicting adversary military potential before it can be used effectively against friendly forces.

(3) Destroying or disrupting critical adversary C2 capabilities.

(4) Limiting destruction within the HN and against adversary forces, functions, and facilities to the minimum required to achieve both the JFLCC's and the JFC's guidance and intent, enabling potential exploitation, or use in continuing or future operations.

b. **Fires Synchronization and Coordination.** The JFLCC's primary agency—to synchronize and coordinate joint fires and their effects—is either an Army fires cell or a Marine force fires coordination center (FFCC) or fire support coordination center (FSCC) of the J-3. The fires cell or center reviews the JFC's guidance and intent, and makes recommendations for the JFLCC to create the desired effects that support achievement of the objectives. The fires cell or center applies this guidance as it shapes the operational environment for the land component's current and future fights.

c. **US Army Joint Fire Support C2.** Fire support personnel are assigned at all levels from company to theater level. At company level, a fire support officer (FSO) leads the fire support team. The brigade FSO leads the brigade fires cell. The BCT fires battalion commander is the BCT's fire support coordinator. Battalion/squadron level fires cells are led by FSOs. A chief of fires is authorized from division to theater level. He is assisted by FSOs and fire support noncommissioned officers.

(1) **Chief of Fires.** The US Army chief of fires is the senior field artillery officer permanently assigned as the full-time fire support staff advisor to division, corps, or theater

army staffs. The chief of fires performs all the staff functions associated with fire support. Additionally, as fires cell supervisor, the chief of fires integrates fire support and electronic attack and related capabilities with each other and assists the operations officer to integrate fires and maneuver into the unit's COP.

(2) **Fires Cell.** The fires cell coordinates and synchronizes the application of joint fires under JFLCC's control. Responsibilities include:

(a) Coordinating and synchronizing all aspects of operational fires with other component commands, major subordinate commands, and multinational forces.

(b) Working in direct coordination with the air support operations center for CAS or through the BCD to the joint air operations center for air interdiction and other air support. It also participates in the JTF JTCB and other JTF boards.

(c) Identify requirements for fires from other components (air interdiction/CAS/naval surface fire support). Influence the JFACC's air apportionment recommendation.

(d) Review and comment on the JFACC's air apportionment recommendation.

(e) Identify assets for JFC allocation (e.g., Army Tactical Missile System/attack helicopters), when available.

(f) Develop JFLCC targeting guidance and priorities.

(g) Integrate and synchronize lethal and nonlethal capabilities.

d. **USMC Joint Fires C2.** Depending upon the mission, and the decision of the JFC, MARFOR may be employed as the joint force land component.

(1) Various agencies and elements are established within the MAGTFs when designated to form a joint force land component command to assist in the execution of their fires responsibilities. The MEF command element organizes a FFCC, which is responsible for overall fires coordination.

(2) At each level below the MEF command element (division, regiment, and battalion), a FSCC is established as an advisory and coordination agency within the ground combat element. The FFCC and each FSCC is staffed with representatives of the Marine Corps and other component organizations, dependent on the mission.

e. **Resources.** The JFLCC's primary means to attack targets are operational fires and interdiction. Potential resources available include Army and Marine Corps ground maneuver forces (i.e., regiments, BCTs, divisions), Army and Marine Corps aviation, and Army and Marine Corps tactical missile systems. Additional resources that may be made available in an OPCON, TACON, or supporting relationship for riverine and surface fire support, include Navy or Air Force and SOF.

See JP 3-09, Joint Fire Support, *for more information.*

f. **Targeting.** Targeting is the process of selecting and prioritizing targets and matching the appropriate response to them, considering operational requirements and capabilities. Targeting is executed and applied at all levels within the joint force to incorporate the wide variety of capabilities to create desired effects and to support the achievement of objectives. Effective coordination, deconfliction, prioritization, synchronization, integration, and assessment maximize the potential for achieving objectives. Decisions to modify missions or direct attacks that deviate from the OPORD should be based on the commander's guidance. These decisions are made with the understanding of the perspective and target priorities of other components throughout the campaign. The JFLCC must have effective joint targeting procedures that:

(1) Comply with JFC's objectives, guidance, and intent as well as with the law of war and established ROE.

(2) Conduct target development.

(3) Nominate targets for inclusion in the joint target list and the restricted target list; nominate targets for inclusion on the JFC's time-sensitive target (TST) list and maintain own list of high-priority targets.

(4) Identify and nominate component-critical targets for JFC approval. Typically these are component nominations not approved as TSTs by the JFC.

(5) Provide tactical and operational assessment to the joint fires element (JFE) for incorporation into the JFC's overall efforts.

(6) Consolidate and nominate deconflicted and prioritized targets for inclusion in the joint integrated prioritized target list.

(7) Provide appropriate representation to the JFE, the joint targeting working group, and JTCB, as well as other associated staff organizations when established.

(8) Provide timely and accurate reporting to the JFE.

(9) Ensure integration of all nonlethal capabilities in the targeting process.

(10) Conduct weaponeering, the process of determining the quantity of a specific type of lethal or nonlethal weapons required to create a specific level of damage to a given target, considering target vulnerability, weapons characteristics and effects, and delivery parameters.

g. **Joint Targeting Process.** The JFLCC conducts targeting within the joint targeting process. A primary consideration in organizing the framework of the joint targeting cycle is the requirement to coordinate, deconflict, prioritize, integrate, synchronize, and assess joint targeting operations. The structure established by the JFLCC must be able to facilitate the joint targeting process throughout the entire spectrum of anticipated targeting timelines from long-term to rapidly changing time-sensitive situations. In addition, the joint force must react to rapidly changing events. Likewise, it should execute all phases of the joint targeting process efficiently and continuously. The joint targeting process cuts across traditional functional and organizational boundaries. Operations, plans, and intelligence are the primary staff participants, but other functional area (e.g., as logistics, weather, legal, and communications) subject matter experts also support the joint targeting cycle. Close coordination, cooperation, and communication are essential for the best use of JFLCC and component resources. **The JFLCC develops guidance that directs and focuses operation planning and targeting to support the JFC's CONOPS, complies with applicable ROE, and submits detailed operational-level schemes of maneuver for future operations to the JFC for joint targeting support.** In the event of conflict of targeting priorities or ROE, changes may be requested from the JFC.

h. **Targeting Coordination Board.** **The JFLCC may organize a targeting coordination board to function as an integrating center to accomplish targeting oversight functions or as a JFLCC-level review mechanism for fires, from lethal and nonlethal weapons.** In either case, it must be a joint activity with appropriate representatives from the other components, subordinate units, and the JFLCC's staff. JFLCC targeting responsibilities are listed below:

(1) To retain authority and responsibility to direct target priorities for land operations and coordinate subordinate units' effort.

(2) To provide clear guidance and objectives for JFLCC operational planning and targeting.

(3) To update JFLCC mission planning guidance, intent, and priority intelligence requirements.

(4) To direct the formation, composition, and specific responsibilities of a JFLCC's targeting coordination board to support land operations.

(5) To review target selection for unnecessary adverse impacts, such as collateral or environmental damage and potential intelligence gains or losses.

i. Subordinate unit responsibilities are listed below:

(1) To identify requirements and nominate targets to the JFLCC.

(2) To provide representation to the JFLCC's targeting coordination board.

(3) To recommend priorities for **battle damage assessment** collection requirements to the JFLCC.

See JP 3-60, Joint Targeting, *for more information.*

OPERATION ICEBERG, THE BATTLE OF OKINAWA

The Battle of Okinawa is an early example of the joint force land component command in operation. During the battle, several innovations, specific to the circumstances of the campaign, were implemented. Among these was Tenth Army's (the LCC) reservation of "the right to assign target and unit priorities, allocating and/or moving assets to where they would have the most beneficial effect on the ground campaign." During the campaign, "Army and Marine artillery were used interchangeably."

SOURCE: Lieutenant Colonel James S. Gavitt, "The Okinawa Campaign: A Case Study," pp. 96-97, Individual Study Project, Carlisle Barracks, PA: US Army War College, 1991.

---

j. **Other Component Fire Support Coordination Responsibilities.** The JFLCC and other component commanders (e.g., JFACC, JFMCC, JFSOCC) develop plans to accomplish the JFC's objectives. **Synchronization, integration, allocation of resources, and matching appropriate weapons to particular targets are essential targeting functions for the component commanders.** All component commanders subordinate to the JFC should have a basic understanding of each component's mission and scheme of maneuver to support the JFC's campaign plan. Therefore, the JFLCC provides a description of the support plan through the liaison elements to the Service and functional components and maintains awareness of other component objectives and plans that have the potential to affect the availability of other targeting resources. This basic understanding promotes unity of effort through the coordination and deconfliction of fires and targeting efforts between components, multinational forces, and other agencies. The JACCE located with the JFLCC's staff provides valuable assistance and liaison from the JFACC and can facilitate coordination in planning and synchronizing operational fires and the establishment and control of FSCMs.

k. **FSCMs** are disseminated electronically by message, database update, and/or overlay through both command and joint fire support channels to higher, lower, and adjacent maneuver and supporting units. Typically they are further disseminated to each level of command, to include the establishing command and all concerned joint fire support agencies. Not all measures may apply to a joint operation. However, knowledge of the various **FSCMs** used by each component is necessary for the effective use of joint fire support. **FSCMs** include permissive measures such as coordinated fire lines, **fire support coordination lines (FSCLs), free fire areas, and kill boxes.** Restrictive measures include **restrictive fire lines, no-fire areas, restrictive fire areas, and zones of fire.**

(1) **Planning and Coordination Considerations.** The establishment or change of an FSCM established by the JFLCC is typically initiated through the J-3 operations cell and ultimately approved by the JFC. FSCMs enhance the expeditious engagement of targets, protect forces, populations, critical infrastructure, and sites of religious or cultural significance, and set the stage for future operations. Commanders position and adjust FSCMs consistent with the operational situation and in consultation with superior, subordinate, supporting, and affected commanders. The operations cell informs coordination elements of the change and effective time. Conditions which dictate the change of FSCMs

---

are also coordinated with the other agencies and components as appropriate. As conditions are met, the new FSCM effective time can be projected and announced. Following direction to execute the change, the operations cell should confirm with all liaison elements that the FSCM changes have been disseminated. This ensures that affected units are aware of new FSCM locations and associated positive control measures are being followed, thus reducing the risk of friendly fire incidents.

(2) **FSCL.** FSCLs facilitate the expeditious engagement of targets of opportunity beyond the coordinating measure. A FSCL does not divide an AO. The FSCL applies to all fires of air, land, and sea-based weapon systems using any type of munitions against surface targets. A FSCL is established and adjusted by the appropriate land force commander within their boundaries in consultation with superior, subordinate, supporting, and affected commanders. The FSCL is a term oriented to air-land operations and is normally located only on land, however in certain situations, such as littoral areas, the FSCL may affect both land and sea areas. If possible, the FSCL should follow well-defined terrain features to assist identification from the air.

11. Movement and Maneuver

a. This function encompasses disposing joint forces to conduct campaigns, major operations, and other contingencies by securing positional advantages before combat operations commence and by exploiting tactical success to achieve operational and strategic objectives. This includes moving or deploying forces into an operational area and conducting maneuver to operational depths for offensive or defensive purposes. The JFLCC is responsible for the operational movement and maneuver of land forces necessary to contribute to the success of the JFC's campaign and directs the land force in performance of operational tasks. **The JFLCC plans, controls, and coordinates land movement and maneuver to gain a positional advantage or a mobility differential over the adversary.** The purpose is to achieve the objectives assigned in the theater or subordinate campaign plan. The objective for operational maneuver is usually to gain the positional advantage over an adversary COG or decisive point.

b. Key JFLCC movement and maneuver considerations are listed below:

(1) The JFLCC normally assumes control of forces from the Service component commander upon completion of their JRSOI in theater. The JFLCC must have the requisite C2 capability to effectively employ the force.

(2) The JFLCC must effectively integrate the different capabilities, requirements, and limitations of the forces and capabilities assigned.

(3) The notional JFLCC's staff organization (see Appendix A, "Notional Headquarters Organization") provides for the integration of staff officers from each Service into each section of the JFLCC's staff. It is essential that each Service participate in the planning process of all movement and maneuver to ensure consideration of Service-unique capabilities and limitations.

(4) A key to maximizing capabilities is to understand the maneuver requirements of each assigned force. This requires detailed and continuous coordination with other components and careful consideration of FSCMs and boundaries. This also requires an understanding of the maneuver environment in which each unit will have to conduct operations, to include how the effects of terrain, weather, and possible enemy actions (fires, barriers, mines, improvised explosive devices [IEDs], etc.) could impede maneuver.

c. The JFLCC makes recommendations to the JFC on the following:

(1) Land force structure and organization for combat.

(2) Integration and employment of multinational land forces.

(3) Land force scheme of maneuver and fire support to support the JFC's CONOPS.

(4) Priorities of effort for land forces.

(5) Designating the FSCMs and AO boundaries for subordinate commanders.

(6) Intelligence collection priorities.

(7) Joint fires to support the land forces.

(8) Joint fires to support other components.

(9) Space support to the land force.

(10) Airspace control requests, coordinating altitudes, and other ACMs are submitted to the airspace control authority for approval.

For more on the theater air to ground system, see JP 3-52, Joint Airspace Control; and ATTP 3-04.15/Marine Corps Reference Publication (MCRP) 3-42.1A/NTTP 3-55.14/AFTTP 3-2.64, Multi-Service Tactics, Techniques, and Procedures for Unmanned Aircraft Systems.

(11) Interdiction targets or objectives within the JFLCC's operational area.

(12) Special operations support to the land force.

(13) Land forces continuing operations in CBRN environments before, during, and after a CBRN event.

(14) Land forces to provide consequence management during the conflict or to support WMD elimination operations.

See JP 3-11, Operations in Chemical, Biological, Radiological and Nuclear Environments, for more information about how to operate in CBRN environments; JP 3-41, Chemical, Biological, Radiological, and Nuclear Consequence Management, for more information on managing the consequences of a CBRN event, and JP 3-40, Countering Weapons of Mass Destruction, *for more information on WMD elimination operations.*

(15) Land forces to conduct the **site exploitation** (SE) of any site with political, military, economic, social, information, infrastructure, physical environment, or time sensitivity to the US.

12. Protection

a. As a responsibility of command, not a separate mission, the JFC considers all elements of force protection. Force protection consists of actions taken to prevent or mitigate hostile actions against DOD personnel (to include family members), resources, facilities, and critical information. Protection may also extend to friendly forces, however designated. These actions conserve the force's fighting potential so it can be applied at the decisive time and place and incorporate the coordinated and synchronized offensive and defensive measures to enable the effective employment of the joint force while degrading opportunities for the adversary. Force protection does not include actions to defeat the adversary or protect against accidents, weather, or disease. **The JFLCC will set appropriate force protection condition (FPCON) for the AO equal to or more restrictive than the JFC's baseline FPCON.** The JFLCC may form a protection cell under the J-3 to synchronize and coordinate protection. US Army divisions, corps, and theater army headquarters have a protection cell with a chief of protection authorized.

b. The protection function encompasses a number of tasks, including:

(1) Conducting CBRN defense operations in CBRN environments.

(2) Providing AMD.

(3) Conducting antiterrorism (AT) operations.

(4) Conducting information assurance.

(5) Conducting DOD information NETOPS and DCO.

(6) Providing physical security for forces, means, and civilians.

(7) Conducting operations security (OPSEC).

(8) Securing and protecting flanks, bases, base clusters, JSAs, and lines of communications.

(9) Conducting law enforcement measures.

(10) Conducting PR operations.

(11) Managing the consequences of a CBRN incident.

(12) Providing protection to people and equipment from directed energy; laser and radio frequency energy.

c. **CBRN Defense.** The JFLCC may need to establish these defensive measures as part of force protection. During defense operations, detection equipment, intelligence, reporting, reconnaissance, decontamination, and personnel requirements will come into play.

(1) The JFLCC should provide subordinate commanders with information from which they can establish appropriate unit defense measures. This system consolidates the most current intelligence estimates regarding the adversary's offensive capabilities, intent, and activities; and recommends measures to be employed to combat this threat.

(2) **The JFLCC's J-3 establishes the CBRN threat level in coordination with the J-2 and JFLCC's CBRN officer.** Once established, the **FPCON** is disseminated via J-2 and J-3 channels. Actions associated with each **FPCON** are recommended, not directive in nature. They are based on current CBRN defense doctrine but should be assessed in context of the unit's situation and mission.

(a) CBRN threat level is not synonymous with the mission-oriented protective posture (MOPP) levels and/or personal protection equipment levels. Threat is only one of the factors commanders consider when determining the appropriate MOPP level.

(b) The JFLCC, in coordination with, and with the approval of, the JFC, establishes close relationships with other USG departments and agencies, multinational partners, and IGO and NGO partners operating within the AO. Networks and other means of information sharing are established with diplomatic missions, country teams, IGO, and NGO partners within the AO. These sources may provide valuable intelligence on the likelihood of adversary intent to introduce CBRN material/WMD and related improvised devices. They may also produce data on the political and psychological implications, as well as military aspects of effectively countering WMD beyond that provided by organic or other supporting military intelligence sources. The JFLCC may be required to provide land forces as part of a comprehensive effort to locate and secure residual CBRN hazards or WMD capabilities in support of WMD elimination operations.

For more information on CBRN defense, see JP 3-11, Operations in Chemical, Biological, Radiological, and Nuclear Environments.

d. **SE.** The JFLCC may conduct **SE** consisting of a series of activities to preserve, characterize, exploit, and disable or neutralize analyze information, personnel, and/or materiel found during the conduct of operations in order to protect the force and produce an advantage within the operational variables to support tactical, operational, and strategic objectives. SE may be conducted at a **sensitive site** which is a geographically limited area that contains, but is not limited to, biometric residue (or remains), adversary information systems, war crimes sites, critical government facilities, and areas suspected of containing high value targets such as WMD or WMD program elements.

See also ATTP 3-90.15, Site Exploitation Operations.

e. **Defensive Operations for Countering Air and Missile Threats.** The JFC establishes guidance and objectives to protect against air and missile threats. **The JFLCC ensures that integrated AMD conducted by land forces are planned, coordinated, and synchronized with the joint AADC.** Normally AAMDC assets will be TACON to the AADC or the AAMDC will be in support of the AADC. The JFLCC may employ the AAMDC to perform those planning and C2 functions. The AAMDC is an Army C2 headquarters tailored for joint operations and is capable of planning, coordinating, and synchronizing joint theater missile defense operations. The commander of the AAMDC normally commands its subordinate air defense artillery brigades and functions as a special staff officer for the ARFOR (or JFLCC, if appointed). For complex integrated AMD operations, the AADC, with the approval of the JFC, may appoint the AAMDC commander as the assistant or deputy AADC to assist in the integration and synchronization of operations across the joint force to effectively counter air and missile threats.

For additional guidance, see JP 3-01, Countering Air and Missile Threats.

f. **AT Measures.** A comprehensive JFLCC AT program will seek to identify and reduce the risk of loss or damage of personnel and resources which may be targeted by terrorists and to develop procedures to detect and deter planned terrorist actions before they take place. These measures also encompass the limited response and containment by local and military forces. For assets under the control of the JFLCC, an appropriate division of responsibilities is coordinated with the JFC. **The AT program stresses deterrence of terrorist incidents through preventive measures** common to all combatant commands and Services. The program addresses the following:

(1) Threat analysis and threat reduction.

(2) Installation or unit criticality and vulnerability assessments.

(3) Threat assessment based on the threat analysis and friendly vulnerabilities.

(4) Information security.

(5) OPSEC.

(6) Personnel security.

(7) Physical security.

(8) Crisis management planning.

(9) Employment of tactical measures to contain or resolve terrorist incidents.

(10) Continuous training and education of personnel.

See also JP 3-07.2, Antiterrorism.

g. **Information Assurance.** Actions that protect and defend information systems by ensuring availability, integrity, authentication, confidentiality, and nonrepudiation.

h. **DODIN Operations and DCO.** DODIN operations are operations to design, build, configure, secure, operate, maintain, and sustain DOD networks to create and preserve information assurance on the DODIN, and DCO are passive and active CO intended to preserve the ability to utilize friendly cyberspace capabilities and protect DOD data, networks, and capabilities and other designated systems.

See JP 3-12, Cyberspace Operations, *and JP 6-0,* Joint Communications, *for more detail.*

i. **Physical Security Measures.** Physical security measures serve to deter, detect, and defend against threats from terrorists, criminals, and unconventional forces. Measures include barriers and perimeter standoff space, lighting and sensors, vehicle barriers, blast protection, intrusion detection systems and electronic surveillance, and access control devices and systems. Physical security measures, like any defense, should be overlapping and deployed in depth.

See also JP 3-07.2, Antiterrorism, *and JP 3-10,* Joint Security Operations in Theater.

j. **OPSEC Measures.** Effective OPSEC measures minimize the signature of JFLCC activities, avoid set patterns, and employ deception when patterns cannot be altered. Although strategic OPSEC measures are important, the most effective methods manifest themselves at the lowest level. Terrorist activity is discouraged by varying patrol routes, staffing guard posts and towers at irregular intervals, and conducting vehicle and personnel searches and identification checks on a set but unpredictable pattern.

See also JP 3-13.3, Operations Security, *for more information.*

k. **Law Enforcement Measures.** The JFLCC may be tasked to assist in the prevention, detection, response, and investigation of crimes within the assigned AO. Security of high-risk personnel and personnel security are other aspects of force protection that will require JFLCC attention.

l. **PR Operations.** PR operations serve to return isolated personnel to duty, sustain morale, increase operational performance, and deny adversaries the opportunity to influence our military strategy and national will by exploiting the intelligence and propaganda value of isolated personnel. As a component commander the JFLCC is responsible for planning and conducting PR in support of own operations and for isolating events occurring within assigned operational area or as tasked by the JFC. The JFLCC should establish a personnel recovery coordination cell (PRCC) to coordinate all component PR activities, including to coordinate all component PR activities, including coordination with the joint personnel recovery center (JPRC) and other component PRCCs. The JFLCC should be prepared to establish a JPRC if directed or designated as the joint force supported commander for PR. The JFLCC's PRCC may serve as the nucleus for the JPRC with other components providing functionally trained PR augmentees to the JPRC as directed by the JFC to represent their component and assist in coordinating and deconflicting their component's PR capabilities at the joint level.

See JP 3-50, Personnel Recovery, *for more detail.*

13. Sustainment

a. Sustainment is the provision of logistics and personnel services necessary to maintain and prolong operations until mission accomplishment. Joint personnel services include synchronizing and optimizing personnel service support to the joint force (mail, religious, and legal support, and finance and disbursement services); coordinating morale, welfare, and recreation program; accomplishing manpower management; strength reporting and managing casualty reporting (see JP 1-Series publications). Core logistic functions are supply, maintenance operations, health services, transportation, field services, general engineering, and operational contract support. (See JP 4-0, *Joint Logistics*, and other JP 4-Series publications.)

See JP 1-0, Joint Personnel Support, *JP 1-04,* Legal Support to Military Operations, *JP 1-05,* Religious Affairs in Joint Operations, *and JP 1-06,* Financial Management Support in Joint Operations, *for additional information.*

b. **Authority.** CCDRs exercise **directive authority for logistics (DAFL)** and may delegate authority for a common support capability. The CCDR may delegate directive authority for as many common support capabilities to a subordinate JFC as required to accomplish the subordinate JFC's assigned mission. For some commodities or support services common to two or more Services, one Service may be given responsibility for management based on DOD EA designations or inter-Service support agreements. However, the CCDR must formally delineate this delegated directive authority by function and scope to the subordinate JFC or Service component commander. A CCDR's DAFL is not intended to:

(1) Discontinue Service responsibility for logistics support.

(2) Discourage coordination by consultation and agreement.

(3) Disrupt effective procedures, efficient use of facilities, or organization.

(4) Include the ability to provide contracting authority or make binding contracts for the USG.

For more information on DAFL, see JP 1, Doctrine for the Armed Forces of the United States.

c. **Staff.** The JFLCC's J-1, logistics directorate of a joint staff (J-4), and force structure, resource, and assessment directorate of a joint staff (J-8) provide critical functional expertise to the commander in the areas of personnel services and logistics. These staffs focus on key personnel services and logistic issues that may have an adverse affect on the land operations portion of the joint campaign. Generally, they manage by exception only. **Routine administrative, personnel services, and logistic management is the responsibility of the JFC and the subordinate Service component commands.**

See JP 1, Doctrine for the Armed Forces of the United States, *and the JP 4-Series publications. See Appendix A, "Notional Headquarters Organization," for more information on JFLCC's J-1 and J-4 staff organization and responsibilities.*

d. **Responsibilities.** Each Service is responsible for the logistic and personnel services of its own forces, except when support is by agreement with national agencies, multinational partners, or by assignments to common, joint, or cross-servicing. The supported CCDR determines if common servicing would be beneficial within the theater or designated area. **The JFLCC will make recommendations about personnel and logistics support to the JFC** commensurate with priorities developed for land force operations. While each Service retains authority for logistics and personnel service support of its forces, the JFC will ensure support is coordinated and integrated throughout the operation.

e. **EA.** SecDef or the Deputy Secretary of Defense may designate a DOD EA and assign associated logistics responsibilities, functions, and authorities within DOD. These policy responsibilities influence logistics planning within the AOR. EA designations are related to, but not the same as, lead Service designations discussed earlier.

For additional information on EA, refer to JP 1, Doctrine for the Armed Forces of the United States; *for supply commodity related EAs, refer to JP 4-0,* Joint Logistics.

f. **Lead Service.** The CCDR may choose to assign specific CUL functions, to include both planning and execution to a lead Service. These assignments can be for single or multiple common logistical functions, and may also be based on phases and/or locations within the AOR. GCC lead Service assignments are normally aligned to Office of the SecDef-level EA designations, but this may not always be the case. Service component forces, especially the Army, are often required to provide significant levels of theater/JOA-wide support to other Service components, multinational partners, other USG departments and agencies, IGOs, and NGOs. This support and other support directed by GCCs are broadly defined by the Army as Army support to other Services. Army theater echelon support units, such as the TSC, normally provide theater/JOA-wide CUL support requirements, but these are carried out by the ARFOR commander and are not a JFLCC responsibility. **In some cases, the JFLCC may coordinate for lead Service CUL support for the land component, however, the authority to direct logistics is not resident in the JFLCC's OPCON or TACON, unless the GCC delegates directive authority for a common support capability to the JFLCC.** The JFLCC's J-4 staff ensures that JFLCC-directed CUL requirements do not conflict or interfere with GCC-directed lead Service CUL requirements.

See JP 1, Doctrine for the Armed Force of the United States, *and JP 4-0,* Joint Logistics, *for a description of DAFL.*

g. **Contractor Support.** Contracted support to military operations is administered in accordance with federal law and acquisition regulations. Contracting authority does not equal command authority. Contractors are characterized by the type of support they provide and by the source of their contract authority. The JFC and planners should identify a requirement for a contracted system or capability at the earliest opportunity, so all contractors who provide support to the theater requiring transportation can be integrated into the TPFDD. Contractor support falls into three categories: theater support, systems support, and external support.

See JP 4-10, Operational Contract Support, *Department of Defense Instruction 3020.41,* Operational Contract Support (OCS), *and DODD 4270.5,* Military Construction.

h. **Boards and Centers.** The JFLCC is not routinely the lead for JFC-level logistic boards and centers. The JFLCC's J-4 normally participates in selected CCDR/JFC boards and centers that are of critical importance to the successful execution of land operations. **The T-JTB, JDDOC, and/or JMC are transportation-related boards and centers that may have significant impact on land operations** and are examples of higher level joint logistics boards on which the JFLCC may want representation. Other boards and centers of significant importance to the JFC include the joint material priorities and allocation board and the joint petroleum office. To ensure proper focus, the JFLCC participation in these boards needs to be treated as separate and distinct from the Service component participation in these same boards and centers. The JFLCC will not normally convene separate joint logistics boards and centers except when needed to coordinate critical CUL support within the JFLCC's AO.

SECTION C. OTHER OPERATIONS AND CAPABILITIES

14. Information Operations

IO is the integrated employment, during military operations, of IRCs in concert with other lines of operation to influence, disrupt, corrupt, or usurp the decision making of adversaries and potential adversaries while protecting our own. As a functional component commander, the JFLCC may have authority over IRCs as delegated by the JFC. With the speed and complexity of today's operational environment, the JFLCC must develop preliminary IO plans prior to the execution of operations in an effort to shape the environment, seize the initiative, transition from combat to stability operations, and enable transition to civil authority. Considering the lethality of the modern battlefield and the multiplicity of participating nations, NGOs, media, and private organizations, the management and distribution of information is critical to success. The JFC and subordinate commanders must weigh the pros and cons of the release, or withholding, of information from select groups will have upon operations and the local civilian population.

a. **While the Army has established a G-7 [information engagement coordinating staff element], in joint staffs normally the IO section serves under the J-3 (see Appendix A, "Notional Headquarters Organization").** Nonetheless, an IO staff officer should be designated. This officer or an assistant will interface with the joint force IO cell to provide component expertise and act as a liaison for IO matters between the joint force and the component. These representatives also may serve as members of one or more of the supporting organizations of IO, such as the special technical operations cell. Since CO can be used for force application, the JFLCC recommends targets in a manner consistent with target nominations for other weapons systems. Service and functional components requesting specific IO support from sources internal or external to the JFC normally should request such support through the respective joint force component headquarters to the JFC IO cell. Service IO organizations (e.g., 688th Information Operations Wing, 1st IO Command [Land], theater IO groups, Navy IO commands, and the Marine Corps IO Center) also may provide support to the IO cell through the appropriate Service component commanders.

See also JP 3-13, Information Operations, *for more information.*

b. **Military Information Support Operations (MISO).** The purpose of MISO is to induce or reinforce foreign attitudes and behaviors favorable to the originator's objectives. MISO have strategic, operational, and tactical applications. MISO are planned operations to convey selected information and indicators to foreign audiences to influence their emotions, motives, reasoning, and ultimately the behavior of foreign governments, organizations, groups, and individuals. MISO must be integrated into all plans at the initial stages of planning to ensure maximum effectiveness. The MISO approval process, consistent with the JSCP, should be addressed and specified early in the planning process. Army military information support forces assigned to a JFLCC will provide MISO planning and C2 for military information support units that execute MISO in support of the JFLCC's mission.

For additional guidance on MISO, refer to JP 3-13.2, Military Information Support Operations. *MISO support to non-US military is outlined in DODD S-3321.1,* Overt Psychological Operations Conducted by the Military Services in Peacetime and in Contingencies Short of Declared War (U).

c. **Military Deception (MILDEC).** MILDEC includes actions executed to deliberately mislead adversary military decision makers as to friendly military capabilities, intentions, and operations; thereby causing the adversary to take specific actions (or inactions) that will contribute to the accomplishment of the friendly forces' mission. The intent is to cause adversary commanders to form inaccurate impressions about friendly force dispositions, capabilities, vulnerabilities, and intentions; misuse their ISR assets; and/or fail to employ combat or support units to their best advantage. As executed by JFLCCs, MILDEC targets adversary leaders and decision makers through the manipulation of adversary intelligence collection, analysis, and dissemination systems. MILDEC depends on intelligence to identify appropriate deception targets, to assist in developing a credible story, to identify and orient on appropriate receivers (the readers of the story), and to assess the effectiveness of the deception effort. This deception requires a thorough knowledge of opponents and their decision-making processes. During the formulation of the commander's concept, particular attention is placed on defining how the JFLCC would like the adversary to act at critical points in the battle. Those desired adversary actions then become the MILDEC goal. MILDEC is focused on causing the opponents to act in a desired manner, not simply to be misled in their thinking. The MILDEC staff officer may be assigned to the J-5.

For additional guidance on MILDEC, refer to JP 3-13.4, Military Deception.

15. Cyberspace Operations

CO are conducted across the range of military operations and CO capabilities should be considered during JOPP, integrated into plans, and synchronized with other operations during execution. Commanders conduct CO to retain freedom of maneuver in cyberspace, accomplish objectives, deny freedom of action to adversaries, and enable other operational activities. The importance of CO support in all military operations has grown as the joint force increasingly relies on cyberspace for C2 and other critical operations and logistics functions.

See JP 3-12, Cyberspace Operations, *for more detail.*

16. Communication Synchronization

Communication synchronization entails focused efforts to create, strengthen, or preserve conditions favorable for the advancement of national interests, policies, and objectives by understanding and engaging key audiences through the use of coordinated programs, plans, themes, messages, and products synchronized with the actions of all instruments of national power. In support of these efforts, commanders and staffs at all levels should identify and understand key audience perceptions and possible reactions when planning and executing operations. This understanding of key audience perceptions and reactions is a vital element of every theater campaign and contingency plan. Real or perceived differences between actions and words (the "say-do" gap) are addressed and actively mitigated as appropriate, since this divergence can directly contribute to reduced credibility and have a negative impact on the ability to successfully execute current and future missions. Attention paid to commander's communication guidance during planning and execution improves the alignment of multiple lines of operation and lines of effort over time and space, which aligns the overarching message with our actions and activities.

See JP 1, Doctrine for the Armed Forces of the United States, *JP 3-0,* Joint Operations, *and JP 5-0,* Joint Operation Planning, *for more information on commander's communication guidance implementation.*

APPENDIX A
NOTIONAL HEADQUARTERS ORGANIZATION

1. General

The JFLCC's staff is organized based upon the mission and forces assigned and attached. Because creating a new staff would be very time-consuming and inefficient, the staff organization will most likely be derived from an existing Service command structure. The most likely candidates are a theater army contingency command post, an Army corps, or a MAGTF (most likely a MEF). Augmentees from the other Services are integrated into the core staff to form the JFLCC's staff. Ideally, the JFLCC and the deputy JFLCC would come from different Services. This construct should be replicated throughout the staff leadership to ensure an understanding of the distinct capabilities of each Service to optimize force employment. Figure A-1 depicts a notional staff organization.

2. Notional Staff

While Figure A-1 depicts a notional staff organization, it is not prescriptive. The practical assumption is that the actual staff organization is based on the staff organization that forms the core of the staff with some staff members being dual-hatted. Therefore, the actual location and specific duties assigned to certain sections (e.g., engineer) and the specific special staff vary according to the organization of the core staff.

3. Manpower and Personnel Staff Section

The J-1 is the principal staff advisor to the JFLCC for personnel management, personnel services, and personnel manpower administration issues. The personnel estimate and the personnel annex of JFLCC's OPLANs and OPORDs are prepared by the JFLCC's J-1. The JFLCC's J-1 accomplishes personnel accountability and strength reporting for personnel assigned, attached, or OPCON to the joint force land component to the JFC. The J-1 monitors current and projected unit strengths by daily personnel status, casualty, and critical personnel shortages in order to determine their impact on land operations. These reports would be routinely provided from the ARFOR and MARFOR component manpower or personnel staff officer to the JFC with copy furnished to the JFLCC's J-1. The majority of personnel services support and administrative actions are accomplished by the Service components through their Title 10, USC, authority (i.e., pay and entitlements; postal operations; morale, welfare, and recreation; casualty operations; personnel performance evaluations; and awards and decorations). The composition of the JFLCC's J-1 will be dictated by the overall organization of the joint force and the operations to be conducted. Basically, a typical JFLCC's J-1 consists of three divisions: joint manpower, personnel readiness, and personnel services. A notional J-1 organization is provided in Figure A-2.

4. Intelligence Staff Section

The primary role of the J-2 is to provide intelligence support to the JFLCC. A notional organization of the JFLCC's J-2 staff is detailed in Figure A-3. The following intelligence-related actions are the responsibility of the J-2 staff.

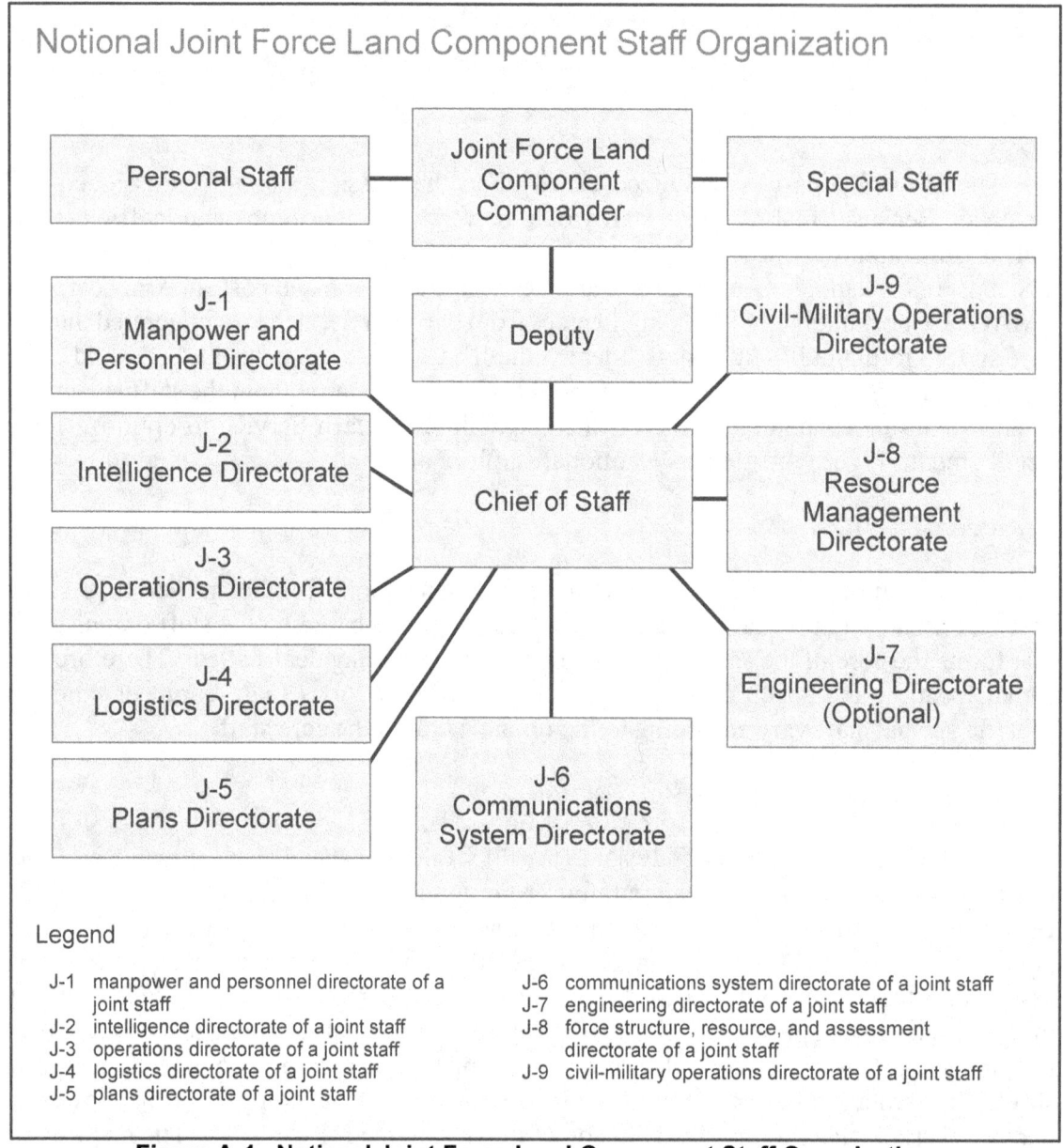

Figure A-1. Notional Joint Force Land Component Staff Organization

a. Provide threat assessment and warning.

b. Participate in all decision making and planning.

c. Synchronize intelligence with operations and plans.

d. Formulate concept of intelligence operations.

e. Develop detailed intelligence annexes.

f. Integrate national and theater intelligence support.

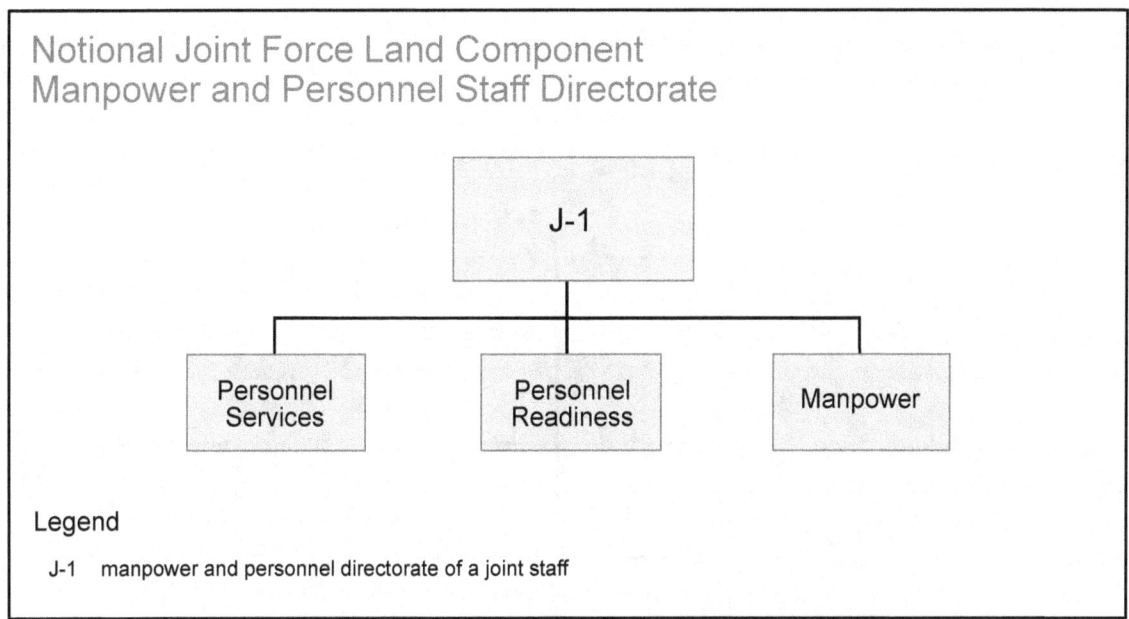

**Figure A-2. Notional Joint Force Land Component
Manpower and Personnel Staff Directorate**

g. Exploit combat reporting from operational forces.

h. Organize for continuous operations.

i. Ensure accessibility of intelligence.

j. Establish a joint intelligence architecture.

For a detailed discussion of each responsibility, see JP 2-0, Joint Intelligence.

5. Operations Staff Section

The J-3 is responsible for the coordination, integration, synchronization, and execution of all operations. The J-3 staff assists the commander in the discharge of assigned responsibilities for the direction and control of operations, beginning with planning and ending when operations are completed. The flexibility and range of modern forces require close coordination and integration for effective unity of effort. The current operations section must have the ability to look out to at least 72 hours for the upcoming commander's decision points. This will allow future operations to conduct planning from the 72 hours out to one week from the current point in time and write the fragmentary orders that direct action based on decision criteria as they are modified by an understanding of the COP. Failure to achieve this standard will tend to draw everyone into the close fight. These sections play an invaluable role during the execution of operations by proposing COAs to address adversary actions or to take advantage of situations. Figure A-4 depicts a notional J-3 staff organization. Its responsibilities include, but are not limited to, the following tasks:

a. Organizing the operational aspects of the headquarters.

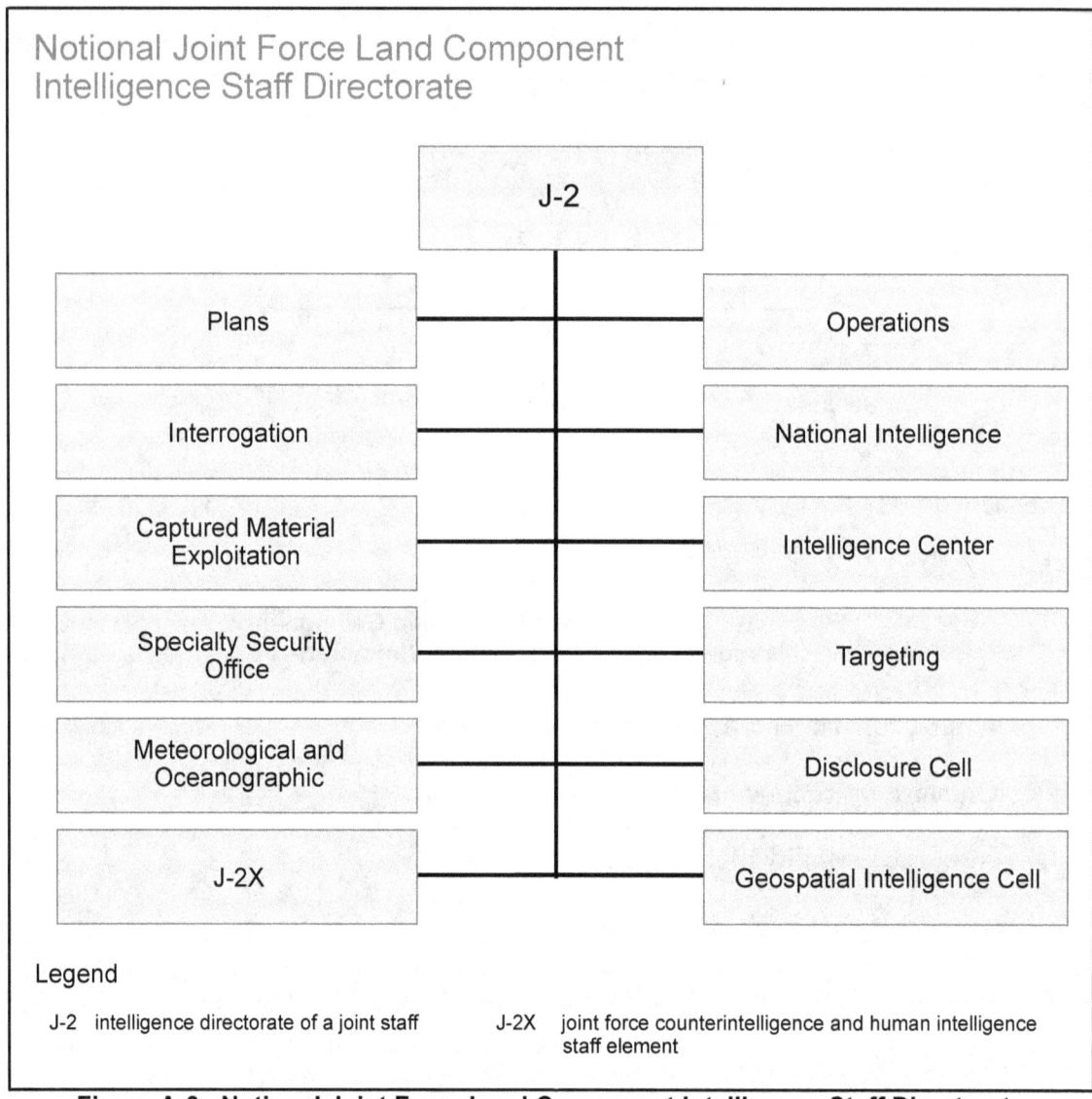

Figure A-3. Notional Joint Force Land Component Intelligence Staff Directorate

  b. Recommending land component command organization to the JFLCC.

  c. Recommending ROE.

  d. Developing plans and orders and exercising staff supervision or cognizance over the conduct of the following:

    (1) Compile an accurate, timely, and complete common land picture for submission to the JFC.

    (2) Operational land combat operations.

    (3) Coordination of operational maneuver.

    (4) Synchronization and integration of fires.

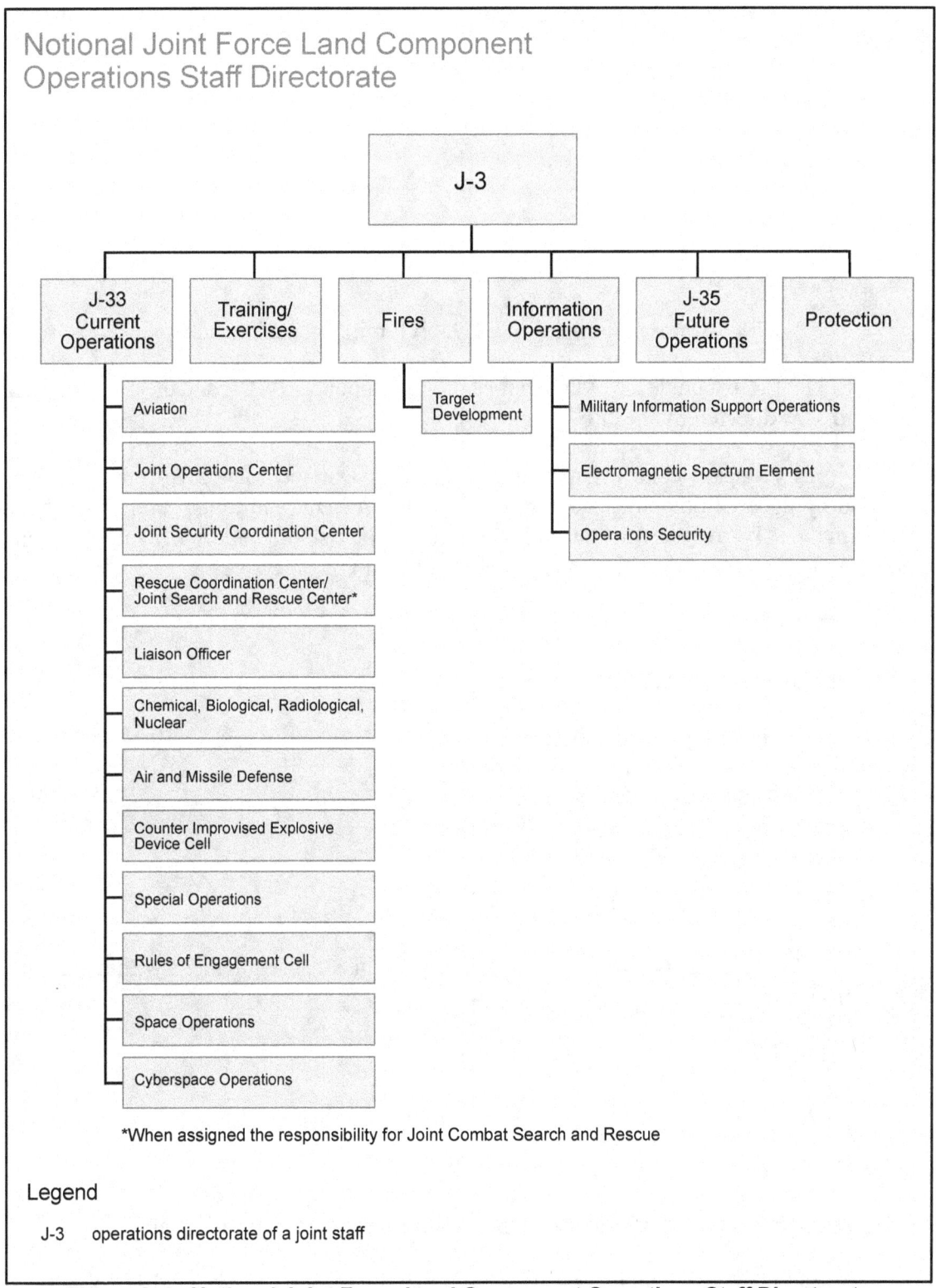

Figure A-4. Notional Joint Force Land Component Operations Staff Directorate

(5) Synchronization and integration of SOF and other USG departments and agencies.

(6) Integration of ACCE (or JACCE) into JFLCC staff.

(7) JSA protection and security.

(8) IO.

(9) Friendly fire prevention measures.

(10) CMO (if not performed by a J-9, civil military staff officer).

(11) PR to include the establishment of the component PRCC and the establishment of the JPRC if directed by the JFC.

(12) Airspace control within a designated AO in accordance with the guidance provided by the ACP, the airspace control order, the AADP, and the special instructions located in the ATO to assure deconfliction, minimize the risk of friendly fire incidents, and optimize the joint force capabilities in support of the JFC's objectives.

(13) ISR.

(14) Space operations.

(15) Humanitarian assistance.

(16) Mine warfare operations (land).

(17) Disaster relief operations.

(18) Counter-improvised explosive device (C-IED) operations.

(19) Establish a component joint data NETOPS cell equivalent within the joint operations center.

(20) CO.

e. Coordinating security of the operations and intelligence center.

f. Coordinating security guards' activities.

g. If established, J-35 (future operations) is responsible for branch plans.

h. If established, J-7 engineer staff section may be responsible for C-IED operations.

6. Logistics Staff Section

The JFLCC's J-4 formulates and implements logistic plans within the AO for forces assigned or attached to the land force. The J-4 oversees the implementation of logistics plans by monitoring the logistic requirements of the components and performs analysis for logistical impacts on land operations. A notional JFLCC's J-4 staff organization is depicted in Figure A-5. The following actions are the responsibility of the J-4.

    a. Monitoring and coordinating logistics functions and requirements.

    b. Advising JFLCC about logistics matters affecting joint and multinational support to land operations.

    c. Preparing and/or assisting the Service component logistics officer on the concept of logistics support for the AO and the logistics annexes of JFLCC's OPLANs and OPORDs.

    d. Recommending to JFLCC, within the guidelines established by the JFC, priorities for the allocation of logistics resources among assigned forces within the AO.

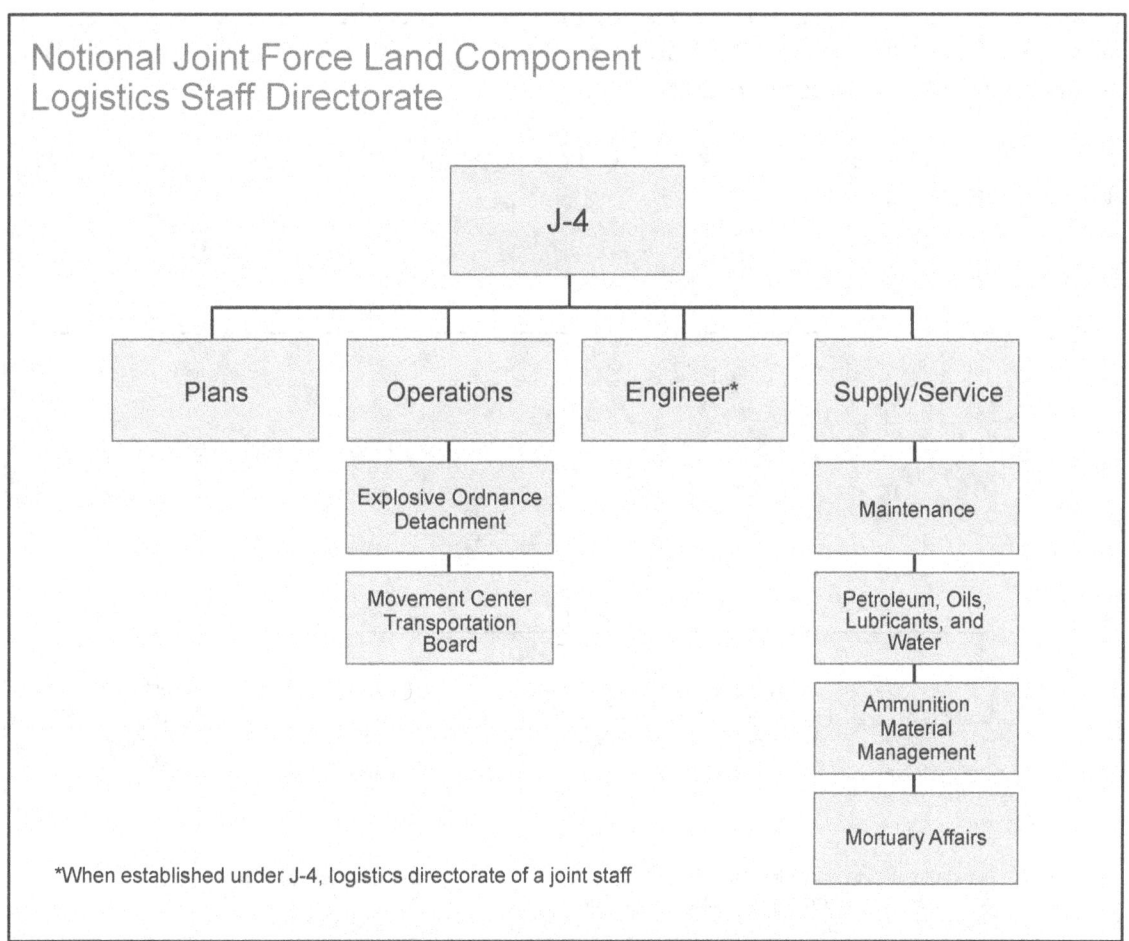

Figure A-5. Notional Joint Force Land Component Logistics Staff Directorate

e. Participating in joint/multinational logistics boards and centers that directly impact on land operations.

f. Maintaining liaison with the other JFLCC's staff, agencies, and JFC counterparts to stay current with logistics, operational, and intelligence situations.

g. Coordinating construction designs and missions for the AO.

h. Coordination of materiel requirements.

i. Planning for operational facilities, contingency bases, lines of communications, mobility, countermobility, and survivability and environmental management (if an engineering staff directorate is not organized separately).

j. Theater organization dependent, maintaining liaison with the ARFOR component logistics staff officer (G-4) and/or MARFOR G-4, and the Army TSC.

7. Plans Staff Section

JFLCC's J-5 operational planning addresses activities required for conducting land force operations. The J-5 future plans section retains its focus on future planning during the course of the campaign—either the next phase of the operation or the future decision points. A notional J-5 staff is depicted at Figure A-6. J-5 responsibilities for the employment and sustainment of land forces are listed below:

a. Employment planning prescribing how to apply force/forces to attain specified military objectives.

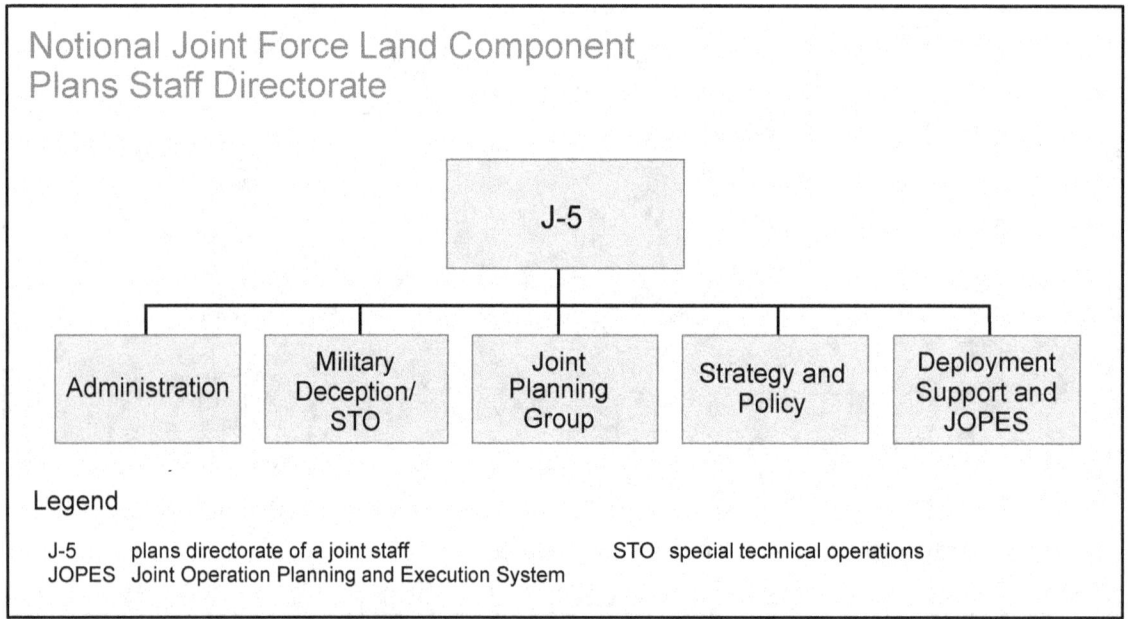

Figure A-6. Notional Joint Force Land Component Plans Staff Directorate

b. Sustainment planning directed toward providing and maintaining levels of personnel, materiel, and consumables required for the planned levels of combat activity for the estimated duration and at the desired level of intensity.

c. Deployment/redeployment planning, including TPFDL development, monitoring the force flow, and the redeployment of forces from theater at campaign's end.

d. Support the JFC's effort in planning the joint operation from phase zero through termination.

e. MILDEC and special technical operations planning.

f. Support to the JFC's security cooperation planning.

8. Communications Systems Staff Section

The J-6 staff coordinates voice, video, data, and message connectivity, cyberspace defense, and DODIN operations supporting JFLCC operations, and gives needed guidance to ensure synchronization between all components and/or subordinate commands. A notional J-6 staff organization is depicted in Figure A-7. The following actions are the responsibility of the J-6:

a. Advises the JFLCC and staff on all communications systems matters.

b. Maintains status of communications to obtain an operational profile of the communications systems network to identify problem areas and solutions.

c. Oversees the establishment of a JNCC to support top-level network control and management within the operational area and gives direction and mission guidance.

d. Prepares and reviews communications systems plans, policies, annexes, and operating instructions, as required, for JFLCC operations.

e. Requests the necessary communications support resources through the JFC's J-6.

f. Identifies communications systems shortfalls to JFC's J-6 for sourcing.

g. Tasks subordinate components for communications systems support as required.

h. Plans, coordinates, and activates, when required, communications systems facilities to provide rapid and reliable communications in support of the JFLCC.

i. Submits request for intertheater communications security (COMSEC) package use to the JFC and issues COMSEC call-out messages.

j. Validates, consolidates, prioritizes, and forwards ultra-high frequency tactical satellite requirements to the JFC for channel allocation.

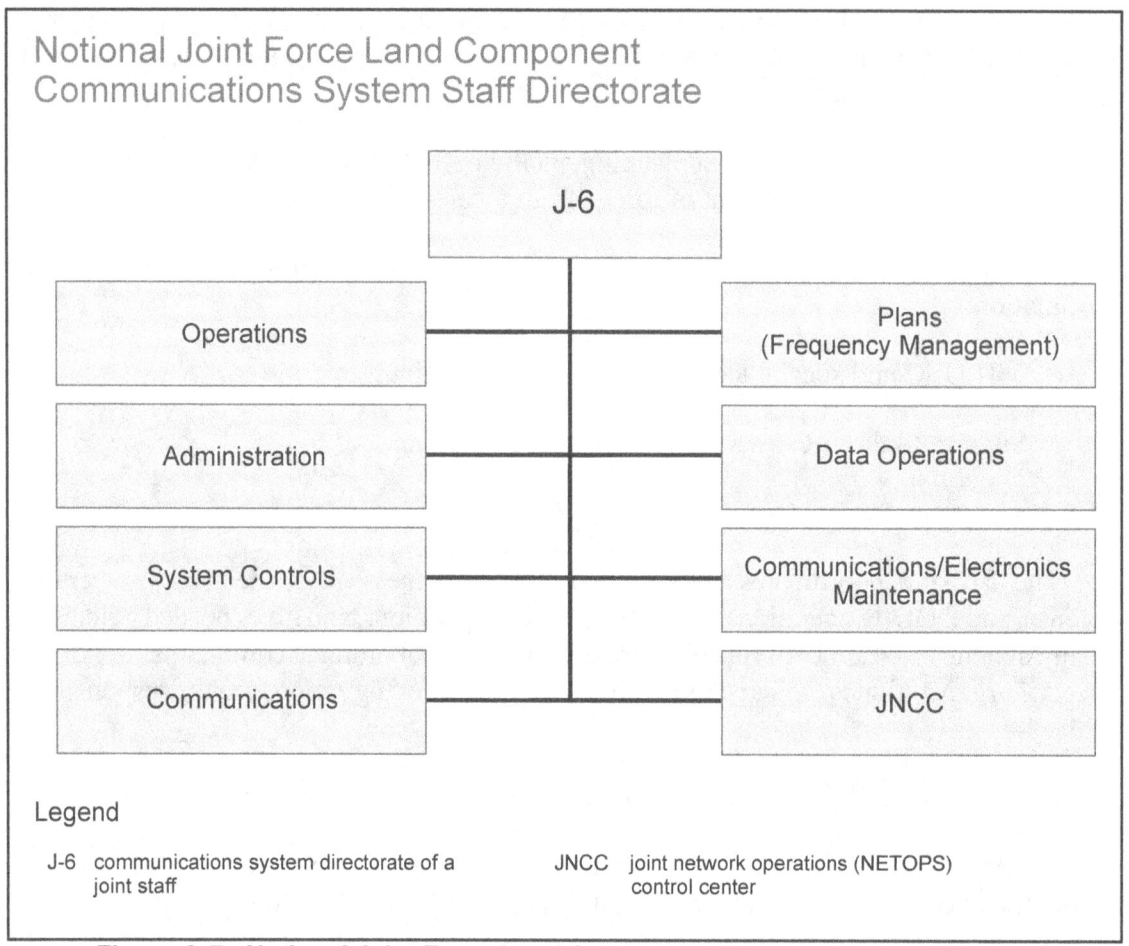

Figure A-7. Notional Joint Force Land Component Communications System Staff Directorate

k. Establishes, supervises, and revises, as necessary, the communications operating procedures pertaining to the unique JFLCC communications facilities.

l. Conducts COMSEC management.

m. Ensures that sound COMSEC principles are adhered to and ensures in-place availability of essential operation codes, authentication systems, and keying materials.

n. Receives, reviews, and advises the JFLCC of COMSEC monitoring reports provided by COMSEC monitoring teams.

o. Develops unique JFLCC signal operating instruction requirements and provides to JFC for review/coordination prior to dissemination.

p. Consolidates and validates radio frequency requirements from components/warfighting elements and coordinates requests with the JFC.

q. Provides guidance and assistance to supporting and assigned forces on all telecommunications and data systems matters for which JFLCC's J-6 has jurisdiction.

r. Consolidates and validates unique JFLCC telecommunications service requirements from components and coordinates with the appropriate agencies.

s. Directs and conducts all communications planning.

t. Determines user communications requirements.

u. Develops critical circuit lists.

v. Develops prioritized listing of systems/circuits for initial activation and provides to the NETOPS center for activation management.

w. Develops prioritized list of systems/circuits for initial activation and restoration, and provides it to the NETOPS center for management.

x. Maintains understanding of future planning direction.

y. Coordinates commercial satellite rights for military systems.

z. Formulates guidance and policy for all communication assets supporting the JFLCC not already addressed by the JFC.

aa. Conducts information assurance and NETOPS as part of cyberspace defense support of JFLCC networks.

bb. Coordinates and facilitates communication support as required to multinational, other USG departments and agencies, IGO, and NGO partners operating within the AO.

cc. Performs frequency and spectrum management for the command.

dd. Coordinates matters related to implementation of virtual collaboration capability and of the supporting CIE that are not in the purview of the JFC.

ee. Develops a list of critical cyberspace assets so that they can be properly protected to support JFLCC operations.

ff. Develops a list of critical infrastructure supporting communications and networks in order to properly defend JFLCC and theater-level DODIN operations fully supported.

9. Engineering Staff Section (Optional)

If organized separately, the J-7 coordinates engineering effort between all components and/or subordinate commands. A notional J-7 staff organization is depicted in Figure A-8. The following actions are the responsibility of the J-7:

a. Planning for and coordinating the conduct of operational mobility, countermobility, and survivability tasks.

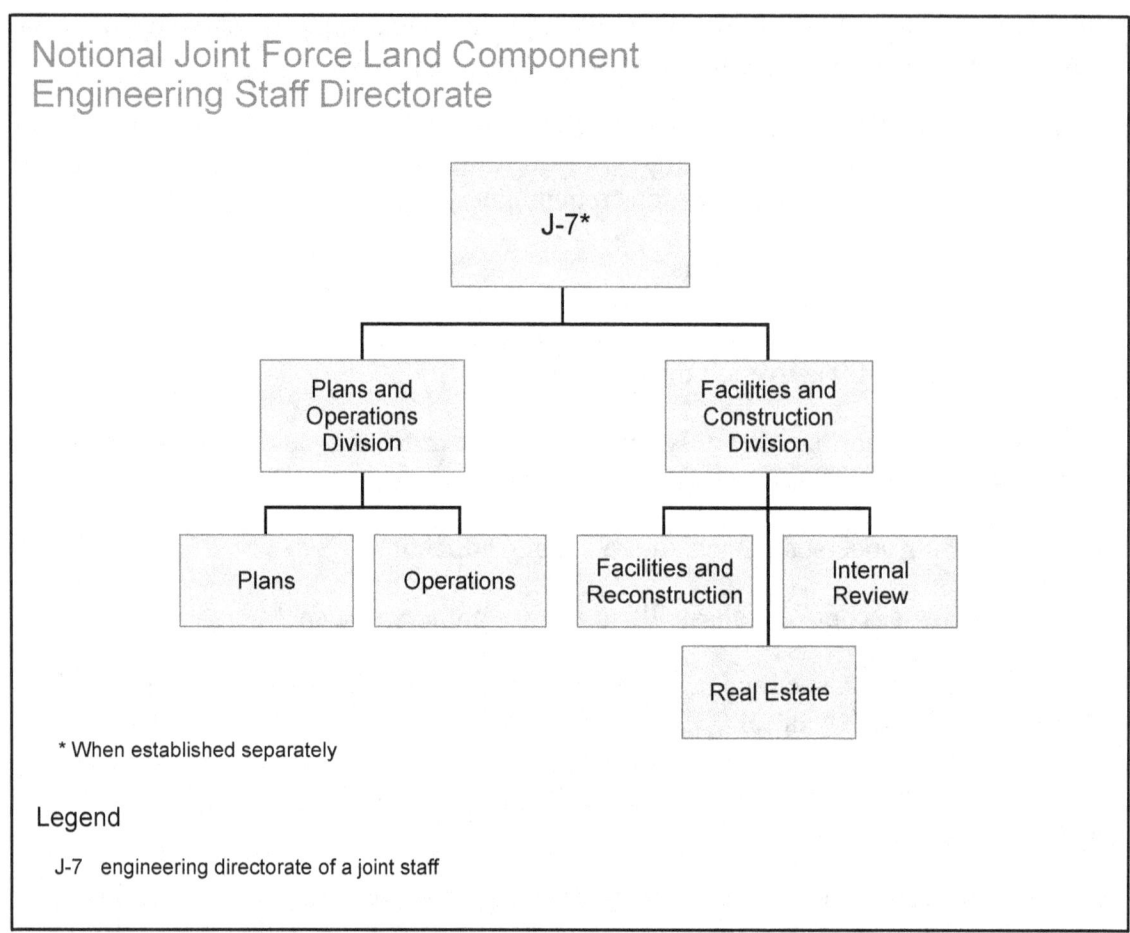

Figure A-8. Notional Joint Force Land Component Engineering Staff Directorate

b. Construction and maintenance of required facilities, contingency bases, and lines of communications.

c. Coordination of Class IV materiel requirements.

d. Environmental management.

e. Geospatial support in conjunction with the geospatial information and services officer.

f. Real estate management.

g. Other specialized engineering support functions.

h. Emergency repair of war damage to facilities and infrastructure.

10. Resource Management Staff Section

The J-8 provides resource management support and coordinates finance operations support. Finance units and resource management capability are staffed separately. Unit placement is within the sustainment community. Each component command establishes their resource management component. Finance operations include disbursing, commercial vendor (contracts) support, and limited pay. Resource management for JFLCC operations comprises fund control, cost capturing, and cost reporting. Commanders and planners should consider cash and funding authority as commodities needed to support force deployment operations. The supported CCDR will identify the designated lead agent for financial management in the joint OPLAN or order. A notional JFLCC's J-8 organization is depicted in Figure A-9.

See JP 1-06, Financial Management Support in Joint Operations, *for additional information.*

a. The JFLCC may designate J-8 with the finance and resource management functional responsibilities listed below:

(1) Serves as principal financial management advisor to the JFLCC for finance operations and resource management.

(2) Ensures the JFLCC exercises appropriate fiscal oversight and control of JFLCC resource management. C2 of finance units resides with the TSC. Acts as focal point within the land component for all issues related to financial management.

(3) Represents the JFLCC in identifying JFLCC financial management to the JFC, component commands, and Services as appropriate.

(4) Participates in OPLAN/OPORD development for JFLCC operations.

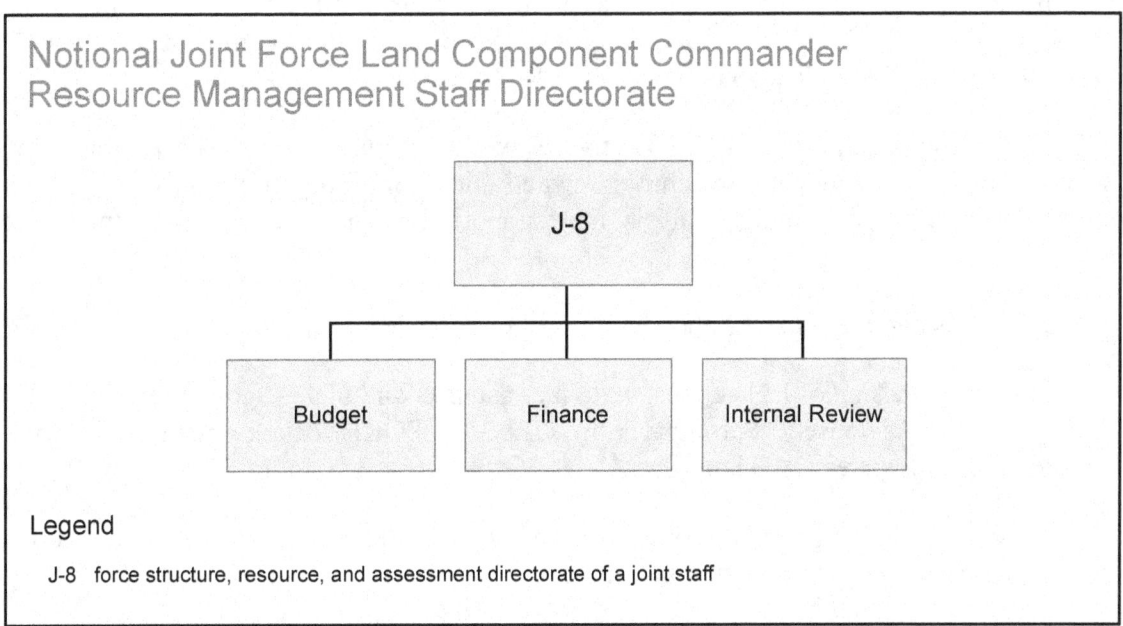

Figure A-9. Notional Joint Force Land Component Commander Resource Management Staff Directorate

(5) Prepares a resource management appendix to OPLANs and orders issued by the JFLCC.

(6) Establishes AO resource management responsibilities.

(7) When needed, coordinates specific resource management functions or special support requirements.

(8) Provides estimates of resource requirements to the component commands, the Services, and the JFC as appropriate.

(9) Maintains positive channels of communication with resource management personnel, the financial management center, the JFC, the Defense Finance and Accounting Service, and other supporting agencies.

(10) Coordinates funding requirements and finance unit support.

(11) Establishes positive controls over funding authority received.

(12) Develops, submits, and validates requirements as necessary in support of resource management requirements.

(13) Develops management internal control processes, controls, and measures applicable to component resource managers as well as relevant to internal staff procedures.

11. Civil-Military Operations Staff Section

The JFLCC may establish a J-9 (see Figure A-10) separate from the J-3 because of the many challenging issues that will arise during operations involving CMO, interagency coordination, FHA, HN support, as well as coordination with other USG departments and agencies, IGOs, NGOs, HN, IPI, and the private sector. The JFLCC may designate a J-9 with the responsibilities listed below:

a. As required, coordinates CMO activities while serving as a conduit for information sharing, support requirements, synchronizing activities, compiling information of the civil environment, and performing analysis that support the commander's assessment and planning needs.

b. Assists and makes recommendations relating to CMO.

c. Plans provision of HN support, nation assistance, and makes recommendations for foreign internal defense. Participates in OPLAN/OPORD development for JFLCC operations and prepares CAO annex.

d. Advises the commander and assists major subordinate commands in interaction within government agencies and populations.

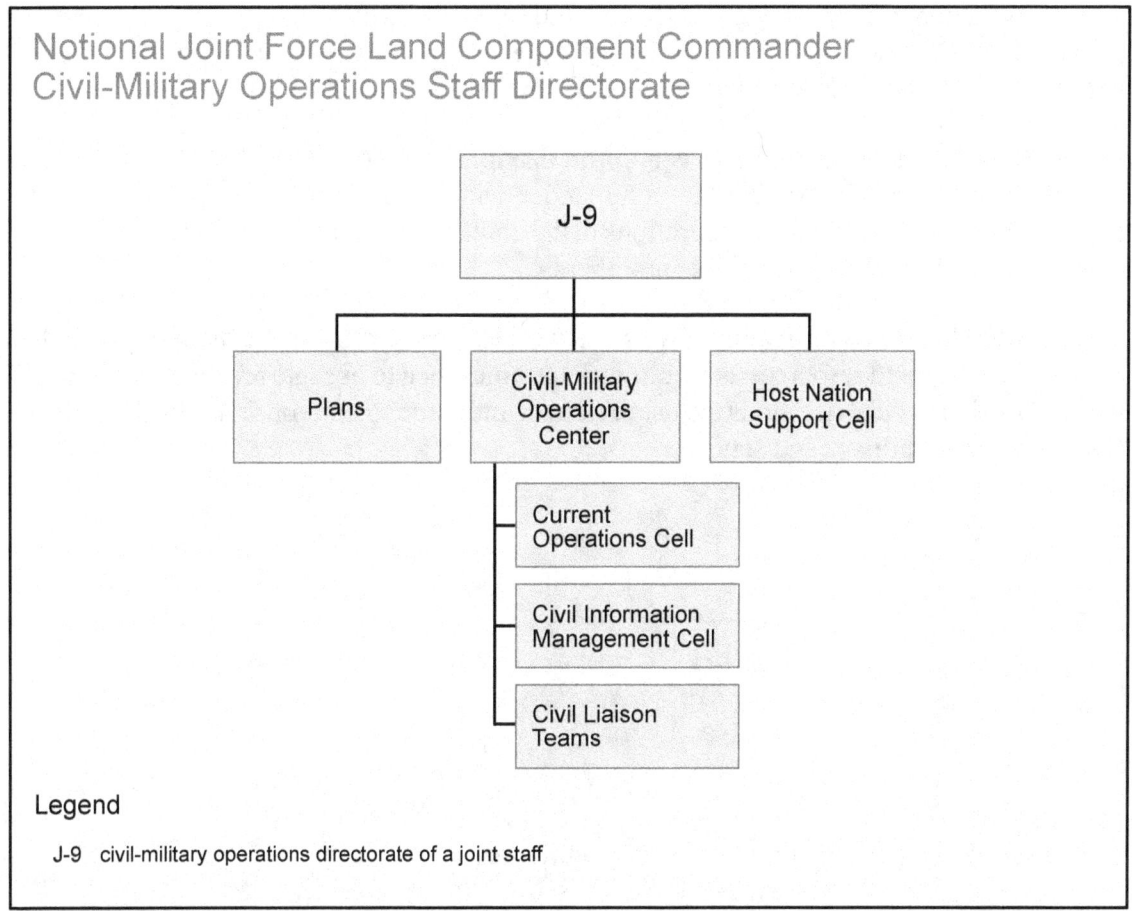

Figure A-10. Notional Joint Force Land Component Commander Civil-Military Operations Staff Directorate

e. Recommends policy for CAO and prepares, implements, and supervises the execution of CA plans. Prepares estimates and conducts surveys and studies in support of CAO. Determines the requirements for resources to accomplish civil-military activities to include CA unit(s), personnel, and equipment.

f. Plans for the conduct of security assistance activities and FHA. In conjunction with the J-4, arranges HN sustainment support for land forces or, when directed, other services.

g. When required, plans for civil administration activities to support the restoration of civil authority.

h. When directed, establishes liaison with other USG departments and agencies, IGOs, NGOs, HN, partner nations, private sector, and IPI that brings these organizations into the realm of planning and information sharing.

12. Special Staff

The special staff consists of representatives of technical or administrative services and may include representatives from other governmental and nongovernmental agencies. The general functions of the special staff include furnishing technical, administrative, and tactical advice and recommendations to the JFLCC and other staff officers; preparing the parts of plans, estimates, and orders in which they have primary interest; and coordinating and supervising the activities for which each staff division is responsible (see Figure A-11).

a. **Red Team.** The red team is an organizational element comprised of trained and educated members that provide the commander with an independent capability to fully explore alternatives in plans and operations in the context of the operational environment and from the perspective of adversaries and others.

b. **ORSA (Assessment).** ORSA assessment actions and measures help commanders adjust operations and resources as required, determine when to execute branches and sequels, and make other critical decisions to ensure current and future operations remain aligned with the mission and military end state.

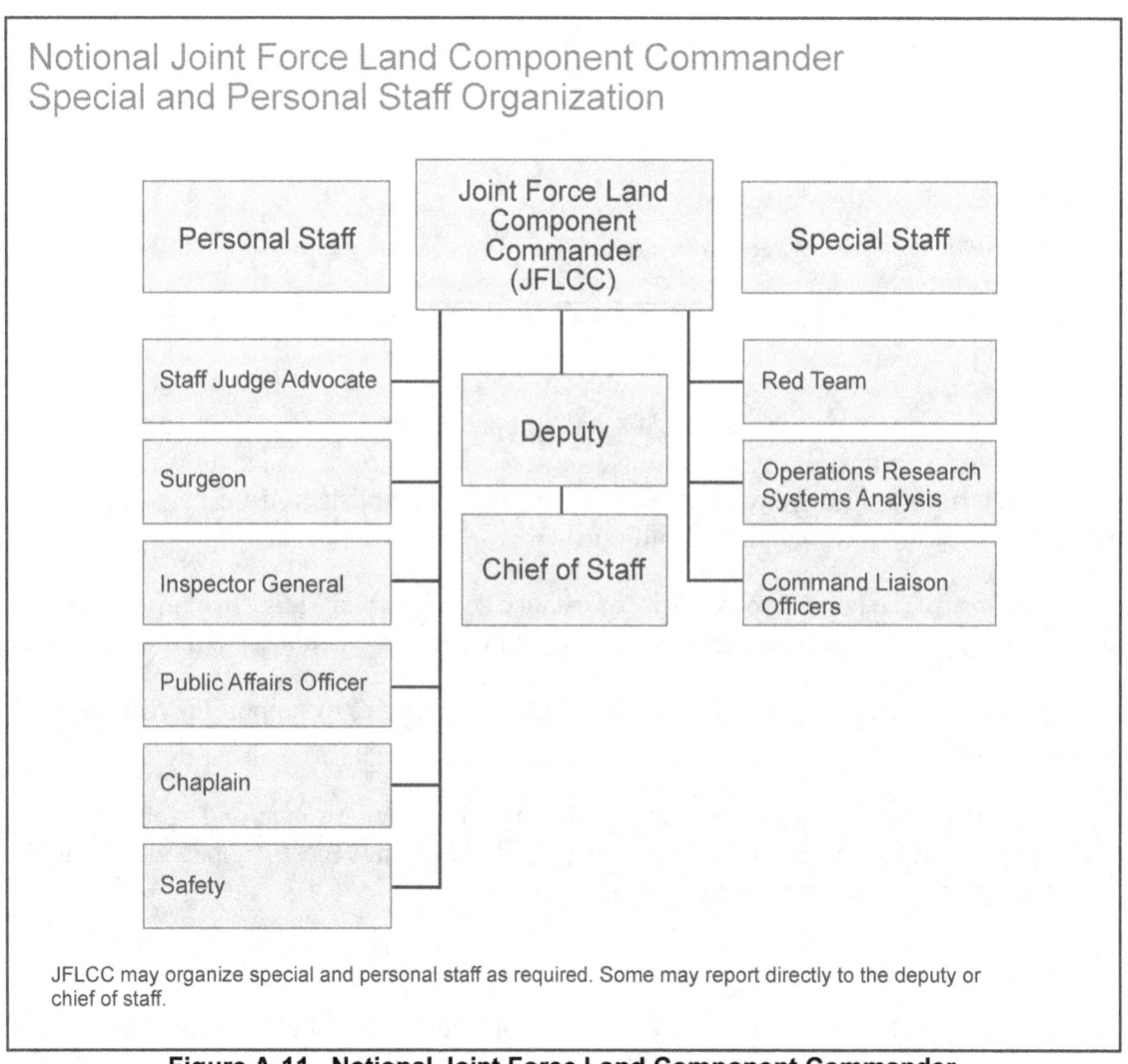

Figure A-11. Notional Joint Force Land Component Commander Special and Personal Staff Organization

c. **Command LNOs.** An LNO represents the commander or a staff officer. The task and its complexity determine the required qualifications. At higher echelons, the complexity of operations often requires an increase in the rank required for LNOs.

13. Personal Staff Group of the Commander

The JFLCC's personal staff performs duties prescribed by the JFLCC and is responsible directly to the JFLCC. This group, normally composed of aides to the JFLCC and staff officers handling special matters over which the JFLCC wishes to exercise close personal control, will usually include a staff judge advocate (SJA), PAO, inspector general (IG), chaplain, surgeon, and others as directed (see Figure A-11).

a. **Chaplain.** The chaplain is responsible to the commander for religious affairs within the command. The chaplain coordinates religious support for the command and provides religious advisement to the commander on matters of religion, morals, and morale as affected by religion, and on the impact of indigenous religions on military operations.

b. **IG.** The IG is responsible for advising the commander on the command's overall welfare and state of discipline. The IG is a confidential advisor to the commander.

c. **PAO.** The PAO is responsible for understanding and fulfilling the information needs of members of joint force, the DOD, and the public.

d. **SJA.** The SJA is the commander's principal legal advisor and provides the full spectrum of legal support through direct and reachback capability to joint operations across the range of military operations.

e. **Safety.** The safety officer is responsible for coordinating safety activities throughout the command.

f. **Surgeon.** The surgeon is responsible for coordinating health assets and operations within the command. The surgeon may also serve as a special staff member.

Intentionally Blank

THEATER-LEVEL LAND COMPONENT PLANNING CONSIDERATIONS

1. Introduction

This appendix provides a set of planning considerations for a theater-level JFLCC.

2. Set the Conditions in the Theater

The GCC owns the theater but the JFLCC plays a significant role in getting it postured to support a wide range of contingencies. The JFLCC typically addresses this mission area through the conduct of the GCC's theater campaign plan strategy as a pre-conflict activity. Each of the Service components leverages engagement activity to strengthen military-to-military and political-to-military relationships, increase the military capabilities of friendly countries, and obtain and maintain access to key nodes within the AOR. A Service component commander must deal with these factors even as the command is transitioning to a joint land force component command or JTF and conducting detailed mission planning and attempting to get key enablers into theater. The JFLCC, however, has additional tasks that must be addressed within this mission area. Their accomplishment will ultimately be key to the entire joint and multinational force should it be committed. Establishing and growing a robust communication systems architecture, integrating JFC CO efforts, positioning Army and joint logistics materiel forward for quick access, investing in seaports of debarkation (SPODs) and aerial ports of debarkation (APODs) infrastructure in coordination with the host countries, and establishing base camps to facilitate rapid RSOI are but a few of the many tasks that the JFLCC should be working to "set the theater."

a. Shaping the information environment has become an essential element of the GCC's theater strategy. The JFLCC must prioritize this effort. IO must be considered the main effort for the land component prior to combat operations as it can and should shape the

---

LAND COMPONENT PLANNING CONSIDERATIONS

Set the Conditions in the theater (Protection, Logistics, Command and Control, Intelligence, Surveillance, and Reconnaissance, Theater "Enablers," Basing/Access/Over Flight...)

Build the Joint/Combined Group Campaign

Receive and Prepare the Forces (Reception, Staging, Onward Movement, and Integration)

Fight the Ground Forces

Assure "Back End" Campaign Success

Lieutenant General David McKiernan, Commander US Army Central Command and Combined Forces Land Component Commander, Operation IRAQI FREEDOM-I

---

environment for joint land operations. IRCs and broad engagement activities that are grounded in an understanding of the people and institutions in the operational area can be significant force multipliers. Use these engagement activities as collection activities to learn as much as possible about the culture and the traditions of the indigenous people as well, not just the military organizations.

b. As the GCC and the components transition to a potential conflict stance, theater preparation tasks receive greater priority and resourcing. There will be a growing need to support Army Support to other Services tasks that will add complexity and further tax limited resources. The lesson from Afghanistan, Iraq, and the Horn of Africa is to work these preparation tasks as early as possible, in a sustained manner and in coordination with not just the GCC but appropriate interagency and multinational actors as well. Resourcing operational tasks to set the theater will be very difficult during non-conflict periods but it pays big dividends should conditions change (to include supporting rapid humanitarian relief operations).

3. Assess the Theater and the Threat

As with setting the theater, the theater and threat assessment is also a continuous process. Experience from Iraq and Afghanistan forced the commands to broaden their collection and assessment activities beyond typical order of battle analysis focused on conventional formations. Infrastructure status, the strength of institutions, tribal and ethnic divisions and hierarchies, and the history and culture of peoples in the AOI become central to JFLCC planning and execution activities. This collective understanding informs a well-integrated, holistic, IO effort. This collection and assessment approach must include the entire land component. It is not a J-2 function alone; every military member is a collector and there should be a reporting process in place to reinforce that. This broader understanding of the mission area is particularly important at the operational to strategic level. Accomplish as much of this as possible prior to potential conflict and leverage every resource to do so, interagency capabilities, multinational formations and liaisons, IGOs, and the observations and reports of members of the staff as they move around the theater. Even as the command transitions to combat operations, this broad collection and assessment process must continue as it should considerably shape post-conflict operations.

4. Build the Joint Land Operation Plan

a. The JFLCC's joint land operations plan requires extensive horizontal and vertical coordination as the land operations will involve a broad range of organizations, both military and nonmilitary. Operations in Iraq have reinforced the importance of conducting planning that addresses the complete depth of the joint campaign—well past major combat operations. In close collaboration with the GCC, the JFLCC must understand the desired strategic end state and then build the joint land OPLAN to either attain the end state or facilitate attainment of the end state. The joint land operations plan should be structured to support a strategic end state, not just a successful military end state. Central to the development of this plan is complete understanding of the higher commander's intent, priorities, and CONOPS. Equally important is an understanding of the other components' intent, their priorities and their CONOPS, and the military limitations of their forces. The JFLCC should make sure the staff is working the land OPLAN in close coordination with not only the GCC staff, but the other component staffs as well. The information environment should be afforded significant energy as the JFLCC builds the joint land OPLAN.

b. Key points for building a joint land operations plan are:

(1) A planning staff that has the right competencies represented, especially logistics planners.

(2) Flexibility. Do not get wedded to any one plan. Things will change, often.

(3) Expect friction with other components fighting for limited theater lift. Make sure the planners understand the priorities.

(4) Get the right interagency and multinational planners and liaison representatives in place early, and use them.

(5) Carefully develop the troop list and balance force capabilities—early and robust presence of protective and sustainment capabilities securing early operational gains and paving the way to strategic success.

(6) Plan for tactical exploitation opportunities and how best to translate tactical success to strategic level success—exploitation creates both opportunity and risk.

(7) Establish the respective roles of the future planners (J-5) and the J-35, the latter responsible for orders development during execution, the former building the joint land operations plan that will be turned over to the J-35 planners prior to execution. Timing is important as is task organization between the two planning staffs.

(8) Treat the information environment as key terrain and shape it accordingly. Efforts to influence the operations from the tactical to strategic level must be planned for in depth, fully coordinated across multiple organizations, and applied with consistency and speed. Use the media to your advantage. Engagement with the press is leader business.

5. Receive the Land Force

JRSOI is the GCC's responsibility in theater. The entire deploy-employ simultaneously construct will likely remain the standard, but it significantly increases risk to mission success and makes it even more important that this mission area be carefully planned and executed. Compounding the problem is the likelihood that the availability of selected APODs and SPODs may not be clear until late in the deployment process. The JFLCC and staff must get involved with the HN, both their military and civilian leadership, to work access problems. The "receive the force" mission set is joint in every respect and requires a joint and fully coordinated planning and execution effort. Another complication is the addition of multinational formations, many of which will not be known until late. The J-4 is normally given responsibility for reception, staging and onward movement, and the J-3 for integration. The JFLCC is involved in the entire JSROI operation, including directing rehearsals. The communication plan for the JRSOI plan must be comprehensive and rehearsed as diligently as the movement of troops and equipment. Importantly, the plan must integrate and fully consider the capabilities, and constraints, of the HN(s). This is a mission area that requires considerable leader engagement as the end result is combat power.

For more information on JRSOI, see JP 3-35, Deployment and Redeployment Operations.

6. Fight the Land Force

At the JFLCC level, the headquarters conducts shaping operations, setting conditions for the corps, MEFs, or major tactical formations to succeed. It requires great discipline to stay out of the subordinates fight and that discipline must be translated to the staff as well. The JFLCC "fights the land force" by assuring commander's intent is well understood and by shaping the operational area with operational fires (lethal and nonlethal), setting and reinforcing key IRC objectives, synchronizing communications, and by sustaining the land force as it moves to secure operational objectives. Concurrently, the JFLCC is managing the force flow to allow for an uninterrupted introduction of additional capability. The JFLCC constitutes a reserve and is prepared to commit it to capitalize on exploitation opportunities or prevent or minimize setbacks.

a. The JFLCC retains focus on the strategic end state, enabled by the objectives achieved by the tactical formations. The JFLCC and the staff should establish a single standard for reporting early in the planning process and absorb the host of requests for information that will emanate from higher headquarters and elsewhere regarding the conduct of the fight. Reporting is key, essential, and requires practice and continuous discipline. There are clear differences between Marine and Army reporting practices and even more differences between US military and non-US military reporting practices. Establish a single standard early.

b. The commander's presence on the battlefield is still a significant force multiplier and no amount of technical connectivity can compensate for physical presence. This principle is as important at the operational to strategic level as it is at the tactical level plan to go forward but keep the entourage as small as possible. Fighting the force includes leveraging the capabilities made available from across the interagency and international organizations that will be present in the operational area, as the JFLCC operates in a truly joint, interagency, intergovernmental, and multinational arena. Maximizing the contributions of each to the advantage of the joint land force will be a central task for the commander. Given the significant interaction the JFLCC will have with these other agencies and organizations, it is important that roles and responsibilities between the GCC and the JFLCC (and their respective staffs) are delineated as each will be engaging with many of these same organizations. This becomes particularly important as the JFLCC engages with interagency and civil authorities that will assume the lead in the post-conflict period.

7. Contribute to Operation or Campaign Success

Strategic success is achieved on the ground, through the interaction of military and civilian entities with the people and their institutions. The JFLCC, supported by the other components, must identify both the requirements and the operational approach to setting conditions that will allow the JFLCC to seize the initiative; facilitate control of the operational area; conduct stability and security; help restore essential services; repair critical infrastructure; provide humanitarian relief; and transition authority to civilian authorities. The JFC supported by the component commanders plays an integral role in determining operational requirements and a coordinated, and where possible integrated, approach to achieve transition to civil authorities and attain the strategic end state. The JFLCC must structure a supporting joint land OPLAN that addresses the complete depth of the operation, well beyond the largely conventional, major combat operations phases. Transition events and stability operations must be fully interwoven into the construct and not considered a secondary or sequential piece. Setting end state conditions begins coincident with crossing the line of departure.

a. Perhaps the greatest challenge for the JFLCC is to fashion a fires and maneuver concept that is at once decisive operationally while equally definitive in setting conditions for an effective strategic end state. Very early in the planning process, the JFLCC must commit a significant amount of time and energy clarifying, with the JFC, what the end state should look like. There always exists the possibility that at the policy level, the particulars of the desired end state and the conditions on the ground, will not have been thought through in any detail. Given this reality, the JFLCC and staff will play a major role in translating broad US strategic objectives into definable, and achievable, end state conditions. Ideally the JFLCC will be given the latitude, and in some cases the authority, to work with other key interagency and multinational organizations in defining and assigning roles and responsibilities for the latter part of the joint campaign. Transitions should be carefully planned for with clear articulation of who assumes responsibility for what, be it military or civilian led. Work hard to eliminate as much ambiguity as possible while retaining a degree of flexibility as conditions will undoubtedly change during execution. But there are some things the JFLCC can probably count on as lead transitions from the military to the civil authorities: significant military resources will be diverted to support civil operations, there will be a large requirement to provide military staff augmentation to the civilian headquarters, and it will take time for the civilian entity to gain sufficient situational understanding to be effective. Unity of effort is particularly important in these latter phases of the joint operation or campaign but is very difficult to achieve as more and more organizations get involved in the transition process. Important to success during transitions is continuity on the military side.

b. The JFLCC should plan to retain responsibility for land operations well past any transition of the lead from military to civil authority—operational experience reinforces the need to absolutely minimize individual and unit rotations in the latter phases of the campaign. Additional planning considerations follow:

(1) The JFLCC must work to set internal command and support relationships that fully leverage other component capabilities throughout the depth of the joint operation or campaign—assuring strategic success calls for the support of joint capabilities well beyond the major combat phase.

(2) Fully consider the impact of operational fires on the desired end state, ensure supporting commanders coordinate all fires conducted within land component AO to reduce friendly fire incidents, and ensure no adverse impact on future operations.

(3) Consider the threat of IEDs, their impact on operations, and the need to stand up a C-IED cell or TF in order to coordinate and conduct IED defeat operations.

(4) Carefully consider force composition and capacity with a view toward the entirety of the campaign—the complete range of tasks to be conducted.

(5) Completely integrate interagency representatives on the staff for planning and execution.

(6) There will generally be multiple transitions in any campaign, many involving other than US military formations. Minimize, to the extent possible, overlapping transitions between different organizations and entities. Executing operational level military transitions, transfer of authority for example, concurrent with hand-off of civil authority from one entity to another should be avoided. Work to get absolute certainty on who is in charge on the ground, what the conditions will be to turn over lead to a civilian authority, and who has the authority to determine when those conditions are met. Transitions, by their very nature, create risk to the force and the mission.

(7) Aggressively pursue a commander's communication approach that is factual, responsive, and holistic. Weave the importance of managing the information environment directly into the commander's intent.

For more information, see US Army War College Guidebook for Joint Force Land Component Commanders.

APPENDIX C
JOINT LAND OPERATION PLAN AND ORDER DEVELOPMENT

This appendix provides considerations for developing a joint land OPLAN or order. SOPs may differ in the degree of detail and emphasis. For formats of actual plans and orders, refer to CJCSM 3130.03, *Adaptive Planning and Execution (APEX) Planning Formats and Guidance.*

1. Situation

a. **General.** The general politico-military environment of the operation that would establish the probable preconditions for execution of the plan include tactical information for phases of the operation. Refer to command and staff estimates, country studies, or related plans. Designate the trigger event that signals execution.

b. **Operational Environment.** A summary of information concerning the AO, which consists of:

(1) A strategic overview of the physical environment, to include climate, geography, and topography. Specific localized information about conditions affecting the early phases of the operation, especially if a forced entry is anticipated. Include weather, key terrain, observation, cover and concealment, obstacles, avenues of approach, drop zones, landing zones, and beach and hydrographic data.

(2) Civil considerations focus on evaluating the areas, structures, capabilities, organizations, people, and events of the human environment. Other considerations include, but are not limited to: urban areas, infrastructure, resources, production, and other capabilities, that impact combat or post-conflict operations.

c. **Adversary Forces.** A description of the adversary, which consists of:

(1) Strategic and operational factors such as the political roots and objectives of adversary activity, personalities, outside support, sanctuaries, logistic capabilities, levels of training and combat experience, morale, strategic and operational COGs, and vulnerabilities.

(2) Factors of immediate concern such as locations, strengths, weapons systems, tactical capabilities, reserves, mobility, and probable COAs.

(3) Information about the military strengths of adversary nations or potential parties to the conflict. Include order of battle information, numbers of major weapons systems, personalities of leaders, levels of training or combat experience, and affiliation with major hostile powers.

d. **Friendly Forces**

(1) Information that may affect the operation. Include mission and applicable higher level, joint, or multinational commander's intent and desired end state.

(2) The roles of other forces, commands, agencies, or organizations that may affect operations.

(3) The organization of the land forces to support the JFC's CONOPS and the authorities provided by the JFC in respect to forces and capabilities provided to the JFLCC (annex A [Task Organization]).

(4) Tasks of supporting friendly forces, commands, or government agencies.

(5) Status-of-forces agreements, constraints, and ROE for the proposed operation with the HN, in coordination with DOS and appropriate embassies and country teams.

(6) For an operation with several phases, any changes in friendly forces by phase in annex A (Task Organization) or annex V (Interagency Coordination).

(7) Commander's Communication Synchronization. Communication themes and messages applicable to the issuing headquarters. (See annex Y.)

e. **Assumptions.** A summary of the conditions and situations that must exist when the plan becomes an order. Include predictions and presumptions concerning the following:

(1) Conditions within host countries and other nations in the region.

(2) US policy for the region such as the application of the War Powers Act.

(3) Involvement by hostile powers, both from outside and within the region, in the internal affairs of nations in the theater.

(4) Impact of US actions in the theater on relations with nations outside the theater.

(5) Adequacy of interagency support.

(6) Bilateral and multilateral consensus on the degree or extent of common threats, for example, the narcotics trade and required actions.

(7) Availability of resources.

(8) Warning times, times, and locations of anticipated hostile actions. The timing of political decisions in friendly nations, the conditions and timing of the release of the use of special weapons.

f. **Legal Considerations**

(1) Determine applicable US and international laws and legal authorities for the operation and incorporate into planning considerations early in the planning cycle.

(2) For domestic operations, such as disaster relief missions, homeland security, and HD missions, determine applicable domestic law and provide legal guidance to

commanders and staff. Further, ensure proper coordination with relevant federal, state, and local governmental organizations and authorities.

(3) Any legal constraints or restraints such as provisions of treaties, agreements, status of forces agreements, and conventions governing the political, humanitarian, and informational limits on the military effort for the proposed operation with the HN, in coordination with DOS and appropriate embassies and country teams.

(4) ROE and/or rules for the use of force proposed for the operation.

2. Mission

A clear, concise statement of task and purpose that clearly indicates what is to be achieved, why, where, when, and by whom for the overall operation.

3. Execution

a. Commander's Intent. An expression, in clear and concise terms, of the commander's personal visualization of the purpose and end state of the operation overall. This links the mission to the CONOPS and guides all subordinate activities.

b. CONOPS. The commander's visualization of how offensive, defensive, and stability or DSCA operations will accomplish the mission. At the operational level, the CONOPS is generally broad in nature, with specified tasks to subordinate units addressed in paragraph 3c (Tasks to Subordinate Units). The concept may be a single paragraph divided into two or more subparagraphs or, if unusually lengthy, prepared as annex C (Operations).

c. When an operation involves two or more clearly distinct and separate phases, the concept is prepared in subparagraphs describing for each phase the specified end state so that subordinates know the intent for each phase. Though listed sequentially, phases are planned concurrently and overlap. The trigger event for the transition between phases is normally the achievement of some intermediate goal. This knowledge will permit subordinates to plan branches within their own plans. The subordinate commanders are empowered to demonstrate initiative in supporting the attainment of the commander's end state. The commander and subordinates can also execute sequels within and at the conclusion of phases, depending on the outcome of battles and engagements. For each phase of the operation include the following:

(1) Movement and Maneuver. Describe scheme of maneuver, as well as the deployment process, to attain initial objectives and the employment of maneuver units. Identify the commander's primary task and purpose during decisive, shaping, and sustaining operations when appropriate. Identify the reserve, main effort, and major regrouping of forces by phase. Ensure stability or DSCA tasks are addressed.

(a) The scheme for forcible entry of combat elements with necessary C2 elements and their accompanying support.

(b) Changes in the form of maneuver or in the nature of the operation.

(c) Mobility and Countermobility. Concept and priorities by phase, unit, or area.

(d) Obscuration. Concept and priorities by phase, unit, or area.

(2) Fires. The employment of fires necessary to include phased concept of fire support to show complex arrangements including priorities of fires and targeting.

(a) Targeting priorities and priorities of fire.

(b) Air support, field artillery support, and naval surface fire support.

(c) Joint interfaces such as the JTCB and the BCD.

(d) Electronic warfare.

(3) ISR. Concept for ISR support and objectives, to include priority of effort, by task, unit, or area (appendix 8 [Reconnaissance] to annex C [Operations]).

(4) Protection. Describe the concept of protection, to include the priorities of protection by unit and area. Address the concept of area security, to include security for routes, bases, and critical infrastructure. Identify tactical combat forces and other reaction forcers. Use subparagraphs for protection categories such as AMD, EOD, force protection posture, CBRN defense, and provost marshal functions (appendix 14 [Force Protection] to annex C [Operations]).

(a) AMD (includes critical asset list/DAL by phase of operation).

(b) Concept of operational security, to include security for joint areas, bases, lines of communications, and critical infrastructure.

(c) EOD.

(d) Provost marshal/law enforcement activities to include detainee operations.

(e) Survivability measures.

(f) CBRN defensive measures.

(g) Force protection postures and conditions.

(h) SE operations to include sensitive sites.

(5) IO. Describe the concept of IO, to include command themes. Identify key leaders and population groups for information engagement by priority. Refer to appendix 3 (Information Operations) to annex C (Operations) and cross reference with annex F (Public Affairs) and annex Y (Strategic Communication Synchronization).

(6) Other significant operations conducted by phase to include annex G (Civil Affairs); annex N (Space Operations); annex P (Host Nation Support); annex T (CBRN Consequence Management); operations with or in support of appendix 4 (Special Operations) to annex C (Operations); appendix 5 (Personnel Recovery) to annex C (Operations); appendix 11 (Noncombatant Evacuation Operations) to annex C (Operations); and appendix 16 (Cyberspace Operations).

d. Tasks for Major Subordinate Commands. Tasks that encompass two or more phases of the major operation for each major subordinate command. Include direct tasks for subordinate units not already covered by phases. Include the initial composition, location, and tasks for the reserve.

e. Coordinating Instructions. Instructions appropriate to two or more units or two or more phases of the operation.

(1) Times, events, or situations that signal the transition between phases.

(2) CCIRs.

(3) Essential elements of friendly information.

(4) ROE (appendix 7 to annex C [Operations]).

(5) FSCMs.

(6) ACMs. Management procedures and formation of an airspace element and its relation with the theater airspace control authority.

(7) Risk Reduction Control Measures. Force protection guidance. Include the MOPP levels, operational exposure guidance, troop-safety criteria, friendly fire prevention measures, and integration of active and passive defense warning systems to include any civil defense requirements.

(8) PR coordination measures (appendix 5 to annex C).

(9) PA operations and guidance (annex F).

4. Sustainment

Operational sustainment instructions are of primary interest to the elements being supported. A JFLCC without an inherent logistics organization will refer to the sustainment plan of the ASCC or other Service components for detailed procedures on how subordinate elements may receive support from Service support organizations. The JFLCC describes those support matters necessary to accomplish the combat mission of the force. If a support organization, such as an Army TSC, is placed under command of a JFLCC, include the detailed information normally found in the theater army plan. Even without an integral support organization, the JFLCC may choose to include the following subjects:

a. Logistics (annex D) to include:

(1) Intermediate staging bases in the target region and repositioning of supplies and equipment.

(2) Priorities of supply and maintenance.

(3) Submission of materiel status reports.

(4) Controlled supply rate for ammunition (Class V).

(5) Designations of lines of communications.

(6) Mortuary affairs.

b. Personnel (annex E) to include:

(1) Reporting procedures for US military and civilian personnel to include contractors.

(2) EPW or detainee reporting procedures.

(3) Labor policies (use of EPW, civilian labor).

c. Medical Services (annex Q) to include:

(1) Medical evacuation policies.

(2) Medical logistics.

(3) Location and capacity of theater hospital facilities.

d. Resource Management to include:

(1) Detailed procedures for making use of labor, transportation, and facilities from HN and friendly third countries.

(2) Operational contract support (annex W).

e. Joint reception, staging, and onward movement of reinforcements.

5. Command and Control

a. Command

(1) Command relationships (annex J). Indicate any major changes by phase and conditions/times for shift. Identify any command arrangement agreements and pertinent memorandums of understanding/agreement.

(2) Command post locations to include location of the commander.

(3) Succession to command.

(4) Liaison requirements. Establishing liaison with the HN, with the higher joint forces command, with other component commands (especially those involved in force projection operations), with SOF already in the operational area, and with appropriate other USG departments and agencies, IGOs, and NGOs.

b. Communications Systems (annex K). Communications and cyberspace defense procedures and priorities such as location of key nodes, spectrum management, communications-electronics operating instructions, codes, and interface with joint or multinational forces.

6. Annexes

Joint land operations plan annexes should focus on the land audience and contain technical details necessary for C2 of all land organizations and capabilities across the joint force. They should contain any details not considered appropriate for the relevant section of the main plan.

A. Task Organization.

B. Intelligence.

C. Operations.

D. Logistics.

E. Personnel.

F. Public Affairs.

G. Civil Affairs.

H. Meteorological and Oceanographic Operations (METOC).

J. Command Relationships.

K. Communications Systems.

L. Environmental Considerations.

N. Space Operations.

P. Host-Nation Support.

Q. Medical Services.

R. Reports.

S. Special Technical Operations.

T. Consequence Management.

V. Interagency Coordination.

W. Operational Contract Support.

X. Execution Checklist.

Y. Communication Synchronization.

Z. Distribution.

APPENDIX D
REFERENCES

The development of JP 3-31 is based on the following references.

1. Federal Law

    a. Title 10 and 32, USC, as amended.

    b. The Goldwater-Nichols Department of Defense Reorganization Act of 1986 (Title 10, USC, Section 111).

    c. The Nunn-Cohen Amendment to the 1987 DOD Authorization Act (Title 10, USC, Section 167).

2. Department of Defense Publications

    a. DODD 3000.03E, *DOD Executive Agent for Non-Lethal Weapons (NLW), and NLW Policy.*

    b DODD 3000.07, *Irregular Warfare.*

    c. DODD 3002.01, *Personnel Recovery in the Department of Defense.*

    d. DODD 5100.01, *Functions of the Department of Defense and Its Major Components.*

    e. DODD 5100.03, *Support of the Headquarters of Combatant and Subordinate Unified Commands.*

    f. DOD Instruction 3000.05, *Stability Operations.*

    g. DOD Instruction 3020.41, *Operational Contract Support (OCS).*

3. Chairman of the Joint Chiefs of Staff Publications

    a. CJCSI 3150.25E, *Joint Lessons Learned Program.*

    b. CJCSI 3151.01B, *Global Command and Control System Common Operational Picture Reporting Requirements.*

    c. CJCSM 3115.01C, *Joint Data Network (JDN) Operations: Volume I.*

    d. CJCSM 3122.01A, *Joint Operation Planning and Execution System (JOPES) Volume I (Planning Policies and Procedures).*

    e. CJCSM 3130.03, *Adaptive Planning and Execution (APEX) Planning Formats and Guidance.*

    f. CJCSI 3270.01A, *Personnel Recovery Within the Department of Defense.*

g. CJCSM 3500.04F, *Universal Joint Task Manual.*

h. CJCSM 6715.01B, *Joint Operational Employment of Virtual Collaboration.*

i. JP 1, *Doctrine for the Armed Forces of the United States.*

j. JP 1-0, *Joint Personnel Support.*

k. JP 1-04, *Legal Support to Military Operations.*

l. JP 1-05, *Religious Affairs in Joint Operations.*

m. JP 1-06, *Financial Management Support in Joint Operations.*

n. JP 2-0, *Joint Intelligence.*

o. JP 2-01, *Joint and National Intelligence Support to Military Operations.*

p. JP 2-01.3, *Joint Intelligence Preparation of the Operational Environment.*

q. JP 2-03, *Geospatial Intelligence in Joint Operations.*

r. JP 3-0, *Joint Operations.*

s. JP 3-01, *Countering Air and Missile Threats.*

t. JP 3-02, *Amphibious Operations.*

u. JP 3-05, *Special Operations.*

v. JP 3-06, *Joint Urban Operations.*

w. JP 3-07, *Stability Operations.*

x. JP 3-07.2, *Antiterrorism.*

y. JP 3-08, *Interorganizational Coordination During Joint Operations.*

z. JP 3-09, *Joint Fire Support.*

aa. JP 3-10, *Joint Security Operations in Theater.*

bb. JP 3-11, *Operations in Chemical, Biological, Radiological, and Nuclear Environments.*

cc. JP 3-12, *Cyberspace Operations.*

dd. JP 3-13, *Information Operations.*

ee. JP 3-13.2, *Military Information Support Operations.*

ff. JP 3-13.3, *Operations Security.*

gg. JP 3-13.4, *Military Deception.*

hh. JP 3-14, *Space Operations.*

ii. JP 3-16, *Multinational Operations.*

jj. JP 3-18, *Joint Forcible Entry Operations.*

kk. JP 3-24, *Counterinsurgency Operations.*

ll. JP 3-26, *Counterterrorism.*

mm. JP 3-28, *Defense Support of Civil Authorities.*

nn. JP 3-30, *Command and Control for Joint Air Operations.*

oo. JP 3-33, *Joint Task Force Headquarters.*

pp. JP 3-34, *Joint Engineer Operations.*

qq. JP 3-35, *Deployment and Redeployment Operations.*

rr. JP 3-40, *Countering Weapons of Mass Destruction.*

ss. JP 3-41, *Chemical, Biological, Radiological, and Nuclear Consequence Management.*

tt. JP 3-50, *Personnel Recovery.*

uu. JP 3-52, *Joint Airspace Control.*

vv. JP 3-57, *Civil-Military Operations.*

ww. JP 3-60, *Joint Targeting.*

xx. JP 3-61, *Public Affairs.*

yy. JP 3-63, *Detainee Operations.*

zz. JP 3-68, *Noncombatant Evacuation Operations.*

aaa. JP 4-0, *Joint Logistics.*

bbb. JP 4-08, *Logistics in Support of Multinational Operations.*

ccc. JP 4-10, *Operational Contract Support.*

ddd. JP 5-0, *Joint Operation Planning.*

eee. JP 6-0, *Joint Communications System.*

fff. JP 6-01, *Joint Electromagnetic Spectrum Management Operations.*

4. **Service, Multi-Service, and Allied Publications and Studies**

a. Air Force Doctrine Document 3-0, *Operations and Planning.*

b. Air Force Doctrine Annex 3-03, *Counterland Operations.*

c. AJP 3.2, *Allied Joint Doctrine for Land Operations.*

d. ADP 1, *The Army.*

e. ADP/ADRP 1-02, *Army Operational Terms and Graphics.*

f. ADP/ADRP 3-0, *Unified Land Operations.*

g. ADP/ADRP 3-05, *Special Operations.*

h. ADP/ADRP 3-07, *Stability Operations.*

i. ADP/ADRP 3-09, *Fires.*

j. ADP/ADRP 3-37, *Protection.*

k. ADP/ADRP 4-0, *Sustainment.*

l. ADP/ADRP 5-0, *The Operations Process.*

m. ADP 6-0, *Mission Command.*

n. ATTP 3-37.31, *Civilian Casualty Mitigation.*

o. ATTP 3-90.15, *Site Exploitation Operations.*

p. ATTP 5-0.1, *Commander and Staff Officer Guide.*

q. FM 3-35.1, *Army Pre-Positioned Stocks.*

r. FM 3-57, *Civil Affairs Operations.*

s. FM 3-93, *Theater Army Operations.*

t. FM 4-94, *Theater Sustainment Command.*

u. FM 7-15, *The Army Universal Task List (AUTL).*

v. Marine Corps Doctrine Publication (MCDP) 1, *Warfighting.*

w. MCDP 1-0, *Marine Corps Operations.*

x. MCDP 6, *Command and Control.*

y. MCWP 5-1, *Marine Corps Planning Process.*

z. NWP 3-02.3M/MCWP 3-32, *Maritime Pre-positioning Force (MPF) Operations.*

aa. ATTP 3-04.15, MCRP 3-42.1A, NTTP 3-55.14, and AFTTP 3-2.64, *Multi-Service Tactics, Techniques, and Procedures for Unmanned Aircraft Systems.*

bb. FM 3-22.40/MCWP 3-15.8/NTTP 3-07.2/AFTTP 3-2.45, *Multi-Service Tactics, Techniques, and Procedures for the Employment of Nonlethal Weapons.*

cc. Colonel John A. Bonin, OPR, *Joint Forces Land Component Commander (JFLCC). Primer.* Carlisle Barracks, PA: US Army War College, Department of Military Strategy, Planning and Operations, Version 3.5, 2 April 2000.

dd. *Joint Forces Land Component Commander ALSA Study*, April 1997.

5. Articles, Books, and Papers

a. Amos, James F., William H. McRaven, and Raymond T. Odierno. *Strategic Landpower: Winning the Clash of Wills*, May 2013.

b. Appleman, Roy E., James M. Burns, Russell A. Gugeler, John Stevens. *United States Army in World War II, The War in the Pacific, Okinawa: the Last Battle.* Washington, DC: Center of Military History, United States Army, 2000. (First Printed 1948).

c. Arthur, Stanley R., Sir Peter de la Billière, Walter E. Boomer, Charles A. Horner, Bernard E. Trainor, and John J. Yeosock. *In the Wake of the Storm.* Wheaton, Illinois: Cantigny First Division Foundation, 2000.

d. Beaumont, Roger A. *Joint Military Operations, A Short History.* Westport, Connecticut: Greenwood Press, 1993.

e. Bonin, John A. *US Army Forces Central Command in Afghanistan and the Arabian Peninsula during Operation Enduring Freedom: 11 September 2001-11 March 2003.* Carlisle, Pennsylvania: Army Heritage Center Foundation, 2003.

f. Bounds, Gary L. *Larger Units: Theater Army—Army Group—Field Army.* Fort Leavenworth, Kansas: Combat Studies Institute, 1985.

g. Casey, George W. "America's Army in an Era of Persistent Conflict." *Army* (October 2008)

h. Center for Army Lessons Learned. *Initial Impressions Report, XVIII Airborne Corps/Multi-National Corps – Iraq.* Fort Leavenworth, Kansas: Combined Arms Center, 2006.

i. von Clausewitz, Carl. *On War*. Edited and translated by Michael Howard and Peter Paret, Princeton, New Jersey: Princeton University Press, 1976.

j. Cushman, John H. *Command and Control of Theater Forces: Issues in Middle East Coalition Command*. Boston, Massachusetts: Harvard University, Center for Information Policy Research, 1991.

k. DOD. *Conduct of the Persian Gulf War, Final Report to Congress*. April 1992.

l. Eisenhower, Dwight D. *Crusade in Europe*. Garden City, New York: Doubleday and Company, Inc.1948.

m. Fontenot, Gregory, E.J. Degan, and David Tohn. *On Point: The United States Army in Operation Iraqi Freedom*. Fort Leavenworth, Kansas: Combat Studies Institute Press, 2004.

n. Gavitt, James S. "The Okinawa Campaign: A Case Study." *Individual Study Project*, Carlisle Barracks, Pennsylvania: US Army War College, 1991.

o. Gordon, Michael R., and General Bernard E. Trainor (Ret.). *The Generals' War*. New York, Toronto, London, Boston: Little, Brown and Company, 1995.

p. Gray, Colin S. *Modern Strategy*. Oxford, England: Oxford University Press, 1999.

q. Hogan, David W. *A Command Post at War: First Army Headquarters in Europe, 1943-1945*. Washington, DC: Center of Military History United States Army, 2000.

r. Luck, Gary, and Mike Findlay. *JTF Level Command Relationships and Joint Force Organization, Focus Paper #4*. Joint Warfighting Center, United States Joint Forces Command, 2007.

s. Luck, Gary, and Mike Findlay. *Joint Operations Insights and Best Practices,* 2nd Edition. Joint Warfighting Center, United States Joint Forces Command, 2008.

t. Scales, Robert H., Jr., *Certain Victory: The US Army in the Gulf War*. Fort Leavenworth, Kansas: US Army Command and General Staff College, 1994.

u. Swain, Richard M. *"Lucky War" Third Army in Desert Storm*. Fort Leavenworth, Kansas: US Army Command and General Staff College Press, 1994.

v. Sun Tzu. *The Art of War*. Translated by Samuel B. Griffith. New York, New York: Oxford University Press, 1971.

w. Turner, Thomas R. "US Army North: Strength in the Homeland." *Army* (October 2008).

x. Weigley, Russell F. *Eisenhower's Lieutenants: The Campaign of France and Germany, 1944-1945*. Bloomington, Indiana: Indiana University Press, 1981.

y. Yates, Larry. "Some Thoughts on US Interventions Since World War II." *Readings,* Fort Leavenworth, Kansas: US Army Command and General Staff College, 1993.

z. Yeosock, John J. "Army Operations in the Gulf Theater." *Military Review* (September 1991).

aa. *Guiding Principles or Stabilization and Reconstruction.* United States Institute for Peace Press, Washington, DC, 2009.

Intentionally Blank

APPENDIX E
ADMINISTRATIVE INSTRUCTIONS

1. User Comments

Users in the field are highly encouraged to submit comments on this publication to: Joint Staff J-7, Deputy Director, Joint Education and Doctrine, ATTN: Joint Doctrine Analysis Division, 116 Lake View Parkway, Suffolk, VA 23435-2697. These comments should address content (accuracy, usefulness, consistency, and organization), writing, and appearance.

2. Authorship

The lead agent for this publication is the Department of the Army. The Joint Staff doctrine sponsor for this publication is the Director for Operations (J-3).

3. Supersession

This publication supersedes JP 3-31, 29 June 2010, *Command and Control for Joint Land Operations.*

4. Change Recommendations

a. Recommendations for urgent changes to this publication should be submitted:

    TO: HQDA, ATTN: DAMO-SSP
    INFO: JOINT STAFF WASHINGTON DC//J7-JED//

b. Routine changes should be submitted electronically to the Deputy Director, Joint Education and Doctrine, ATTN: Joint Doctrine Analysis Division, 116 Lake View Parkway, Suffolk, VA 23435-2697, and info the lead agent and the Director for Joint Force Development, J-7/JED.

c. When a Joint Staff directorate submits a proposal to the Chairman of the Joint Chiefs of Staff that would change source document information reflected in this publication, that directorate will include a proposed change to this publication as an enclosure to its proposal. The Services and other organizations are requested to notify the Joint Staff J-7 when changes to source documents reflected in this publication are initiated.

5. Distribution of Publications

Local reproduction is authorized and access to unclassified publications is unrestricted. However, access to and reproduction authorization for classified JPs must be in accordance with DOD Manual 5200.1, Volume 1, *DOD Information Security Program: Overview, Classification, and Declassification,* and DOD Manual 5200.01, Volume 3, *DOD Information Security Program: Protection of Classified Information.*

6. Distribution of Electronic Publications

a. Joint Staff J-7 will not print copies of JPs for distribution. Electronic versions are available on JDEIS Joint Electronic Library Plus (JEL+) at https://jdeis.js.mil/jdeis/index.jsp (NIPRNET) and http://jdeis.js.smil.mil/jdeis/index.jsp (SIPRNET), and on the JEL at http://www.dtic.mil/doctrine (NIPRNET).

b. Only approved JPs are releasable outside the combatant commands, Services, and Joint Staff. Release of any classified JP to foreign governments or foreign nationals must be requested through the local embassy (Defense Attaché Office) to DIA, Defense Foreign Liaison PO-FL, Room 1E811, 7400 Pentagon, Washington, DC 20301-7400.

c. JEL CD-ROM. Upon request of a joint doctrine development community member, the Joint Staff J-7 will produce and deliver one CD-ROM with current JPs. This JEL CD-ROM will be updated not less than semi-annually and when received can be locally reproduced for use within the combatant commands, Services, and combat support agencies.

GLOSSARY
PART I—ABBREVIATIONS AND ACRONYMS

AADC	area air defense commander
AADP	area air defense plan
AAMDC	United States Army Air and Missile Defense Command
ACCE	air component coordination element
ACM	airspace coordinating measure
ACP	airspace control plan
ADCON	administrative control
ADP	Army doctrine publication
ADRP	Army doctrine reference publication
AFTTP	Air Force tactics, techniques, and procedures
AJP	allied joint publication
AMD	air and missile defense
AO	area of operations
AOI	area of interest
AOR	area of responsibility
APOD	aerial port of debarkation
APS	Army pre-positioned stocks
ARCENT	United States Army Central Command
ARFOR	Army forces
ASCC	Army Service component command
AT	antiterrorism
ATO	air tasking order
ATTP	Army tactics, techniques, and procedures
BCD	battlefield coordination detachment
BCT	brigade combat team
C2	command and control
CA	civil affairs
CAO	civil affairs operations
CAS	close air support
CBRN	chemical, biological, radiological, and nuclear
CCDR	combatant commander
CCIR	commander's critical information requirement
CDRUSSTRATCOM	Commander, United States Strategic Command
CFLCC	coalition forces land component commander
CI	counterintelligence
CIE	collaborative information environment
C-IED	counter-improvised explosive device
CJCSI	Chairman of the Joint Chiefs of Staff instruction
CJCSM	Chairman of the Joint Chiefs of Staff manual
CMO	civil-military operations
CMOC	civil-military operations center

CO	cyberspace operations
COA	course of action
COG	center of gravity
COIN	counterinsurgency
COMSEC	communications security
CONOPS	concept of operations
CONPLAN	operation plan in concept format
COP	common operational picture
CUL	common-user logistics
DAFL	directive authority for logistics
DAL	defended asset list
DCO	defensive cyberspace operations
DHS	Department of Homeland Security
DLD	digital liaison detachment
DOD	Department of Defense
DODD	Department of Defense directive
DODIN	Department of Defense information networks
DOS	Department of State
DSCA	defense support of civil authorities
EA	executive agent
EMS	electromagnetic spectrum
EOD	explosive ordnance disposal
EPW	enemy prisoner of war
FFCC	force fires coordination center (USMC)
FHA	foreign humanitarian assistance
FM	field manual (Army)
FPCON	force protection condition
FSCC	fire support coordination center (USMC)
FSCL	fire support coordination line
FSCM	fire support coordination measure
FSO	fire support officer
G-4	Army or Marine Corps component logistics staff officer (Army division or higher staff, Marine Corps brigade or higher staff)
GCC	geographic combatant commander
GPS	Global Positioning System
HD	homeland defense
HN	host nation
IED	improvised explosive device
IG	inspector general

IGO	intergovernmental organization
IO	information operations
IPI	indigenous populations and institutions
IRC	information-related capability
ISR	intelligence, surveillance, and reconnaissance
IW	irregular warfare
J-1	manpower and personnel directorate of a joint staff
J-2	intelligence directorate of a joint staff
J-3	operations directorate of a joint staff
J-4	logistics directorate of a joint staff
J-5	plans directorate of a joint staff
J-6	communications system directorate of a joint staff
J-7	engineering staff section of a joint staff
J-8	force structure, resource, and assessment directorate of a joint staff
J-9	civil-military operations directorate of a joint staff
J-35	future operations cell
JACCE	joint air component coordination element
JDDOC	joint deployment and distribution operations center
JECC	Joint Enabling Capabilities Command (USTRANSCOM)
JFACC	joint force air component commander
JFC	joint force commander
JFE	joint fires element
JFLCC	joint force land component commander
JFMCC	joint force maritime component commander
JFSOCC	joint force special operations component commander
JIACG	joint interagency coordination group
JIPOE	joint intelligence preparation of the operational environment
JMC	joint movement center
JNCC	joint network operations control center
JOA	joint operations area
JOPP	joint operation planning process
JP	joint publication
JPG	joint planning group
JPRC	joint personnel recovery center
JRSOI	joint reception, staging, onward movement, and integration
JSA	joint security area
JSC	joint security coordinator
JSCP	Joint Strategic Capabilities Plan
JTCB	joint targeting coordination board
JTF	joint task force

LCC	land component commander
LNO	liaison officer
MAGTF	Marine air-ground task force
MARFOR	Marine Corps forces
MCDP	Marine Corps doctrine publication
MCRP	Marine Corps reference publication
MCWP	Marine Corps warfighting publication
MEB	Marine expeditionary brigade
MEF	Marine expeditionary force
MILDEC	military deception
MISO	military information support operations
MOE	measure of effectiveness
MOPP	mission-oriented protective posture
MPF	maritime pre-positioning force
NATO	North Atlantic Treaty Organization
NECC	Navy Expeditionary Combat Command
NETOPS	network operations
NGO	nongovernmental organization
NTTP	Navy tactics, techniques, and procedures
NWP	Navy warfare publication
OEF	Operation ENDURING FREEDOM
OIF	Operation IRAQI FREEDOM
OPCON	operational control
OPLAN	operation plan
OPORD	operation order
OPSEC	operations security
ORSA	operations research and systems analysis
PA	public affairs
PAO	public affairs officer
PR	personnel recovery
PRCC	personnel recovery coordination cell
RFA	request for assistance
RFC	request for capabilities
RFF	request for forces
ROE	rules of engagement
RSOI	reception, staging, onward movement, and integration
SCA	space coordinating authority
SE	site exploitation
SecDef	Secretary of Defense
SJA	staff judge advocate

SJFHQ-E	standing joint force headquarters – elimination
SOF	special operations forces
SOP	standard operating procedure
SPOD	seaport of debarkation
TACON	tactical control
TEC	theater engineer command
TF	task force
T-JTB	theater-joint transportation board
TPFDD	time-phased force and deployment data
TPFDL	time-phased force and deployment list
TSC	theater sustainment command (Army)
TST	time-sensitive target
USC	United States Code
USCENTCOM	United States Central Command
USG	United States Government
USMC	United States Marine Corps
USSOCOM	United States Special Operations Command
WMD	weapons of mass destruction

ammunition controlled supply rate. None. (Approved for removal from JP 1-02.)

Army corps. An intermediate headquarters between divisions and the theater army consisting of two or more divisions together with supporting brigades. (Approved for incorporation into JP 1-02.)

Army Service component command. Command responsible for recommendations to the joint force commander on the allocation and employment of Army forces within a combatant command. Also called **ASCC.** (JP 1-02. SOURCE: JP 3-31)

Army support area. The specific support area for a theater Army that is outside of a division or corps's operational area established primarily for the positioning, employment, and protection of theater support units; and where the majority of the sustaining operations occur. (JP 1-02. SOURCE: JP 3-31)

brigade combat team. A combined arms team that forms the basic building block of the Army's tactical formations. Also called **BCT.** (Approved for incorporation into JP 1-02.)

close support. The action of the supporting force against targets or objectives that are sufficiently near the supported force as to require detailed integration or coordination of the supporting action. (Approved for incorporation into JP 1-02.)

joint land operations. Land operations performed across the range of military operations with land forces made available by Service components in support of the joint force commander's operation or campaign objectives, or in support of other components of the joint force. (JP 1-02. SOURCE: JP 3-31)

joint land operations plan. A plan for a connected series of joint land operations to achieve the joint force commander's objectives within a given time and operational area. (JP 1-02. SOURCE: JP 3-31)

land control operations. The employment of land forces, supported by maritime and air forces (as appropriate) to control vital land areas. (Approved for incorporation into JP 1-02.)

land domain. The area of the Earth's surface ending at the high water mark and overlapping with the maritime domain in the landward segment of the littorals. (Approved for inclusion in JP 1-02.)

land forces. Personnel, weapon systems, vehicles, and support elements operating on land to accomplish assigned missions and tasks. (JP 1-02. SOURCE: JP 3-31)

line of departure. 1. In land warfare, a line designated to coordinate the departure of attack elements. Also called **LD.** (JP 3-31) 2. In amphibious warfare, a suitably marked offshore coordinating line to assist assault craft to land on designated beaches at scheduled times the seaward end of a boat lane. Also called **LOD.** (JP 1-02. SOURCE: JP 3-02)

mission command. The conduct of military operations through decentralized execution based upon mission-type orders. (JP 1-02. SOURCE: JP 3-31)

mutual support. That support which units render each other against an enemy, because of their assigned tasks, their position relative to each other and to the enemy, and their inherent capabilities. (JP 1-02. SOURCE: JP 3-31)

operations research. The analytical study of military problems undertaken to provide responsible commanders and staff agencies with a scientific basis for decision on action to improve military operations. Also called **operational research; operations analysis.** (Approved for incorporation into JP 1-02 with JP 3-31 as the source JP.)

sensitive site. A geographically limited area that contains, but is not limited to, adversary information systems, war crimes sites, critical government facilities, and areas suspected of containing high value targets. (JP 1-02. SOURCE: JP 3-31)

site exploitation. A series of activities to recognize, collect, process, preserve, and analyze information, personnel, and/or materiel found during the conduct of operations. Also called **SE.** (JP 1-02. SOURCE: JP 3-31)

standard operating procedure. A set of instructions applicable to those features of operations that lend themselves to a definite or standardized procedure without loss of effectiveness. Also called **SOP; standing operating procedure.** (Approved for incorporation into JP 1-02.)

standing operating procedure. None. (Approved for removal from JP 1-02.)

Intentionally Blank

JOINT DOCTRINE PUBLICATIONS HIERARCHY

JP 1
JOINT DOCTRINE
JP 1-0
PERSONNEL
JP 2-0
INTELLIGENCE
JP 3-0
OPERATIONS
JP 4-0
LOGISTICS
JP 5-0
PLANS
JP 6-0
COMMUNICATIONS SYSTEM

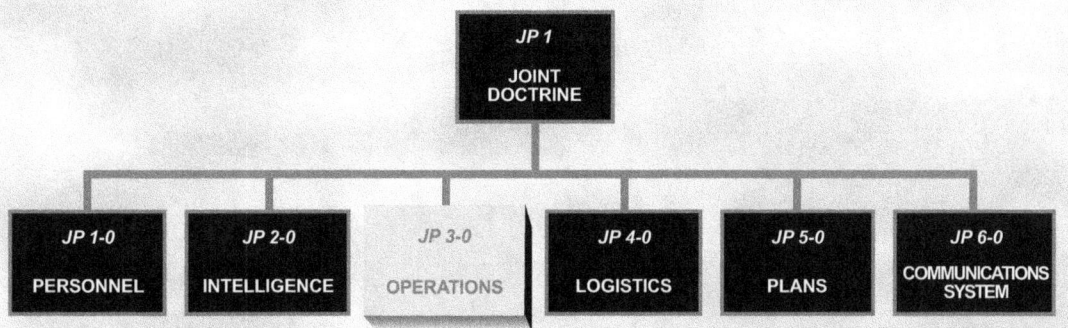

All joint publications are organized into a comprehensive hierarchy as shown in the chart above. **Joint Publication (JP) 3-31** is in the **Operations** series of joint doctrine publications. The diagram below illustrates an overview of the development process:

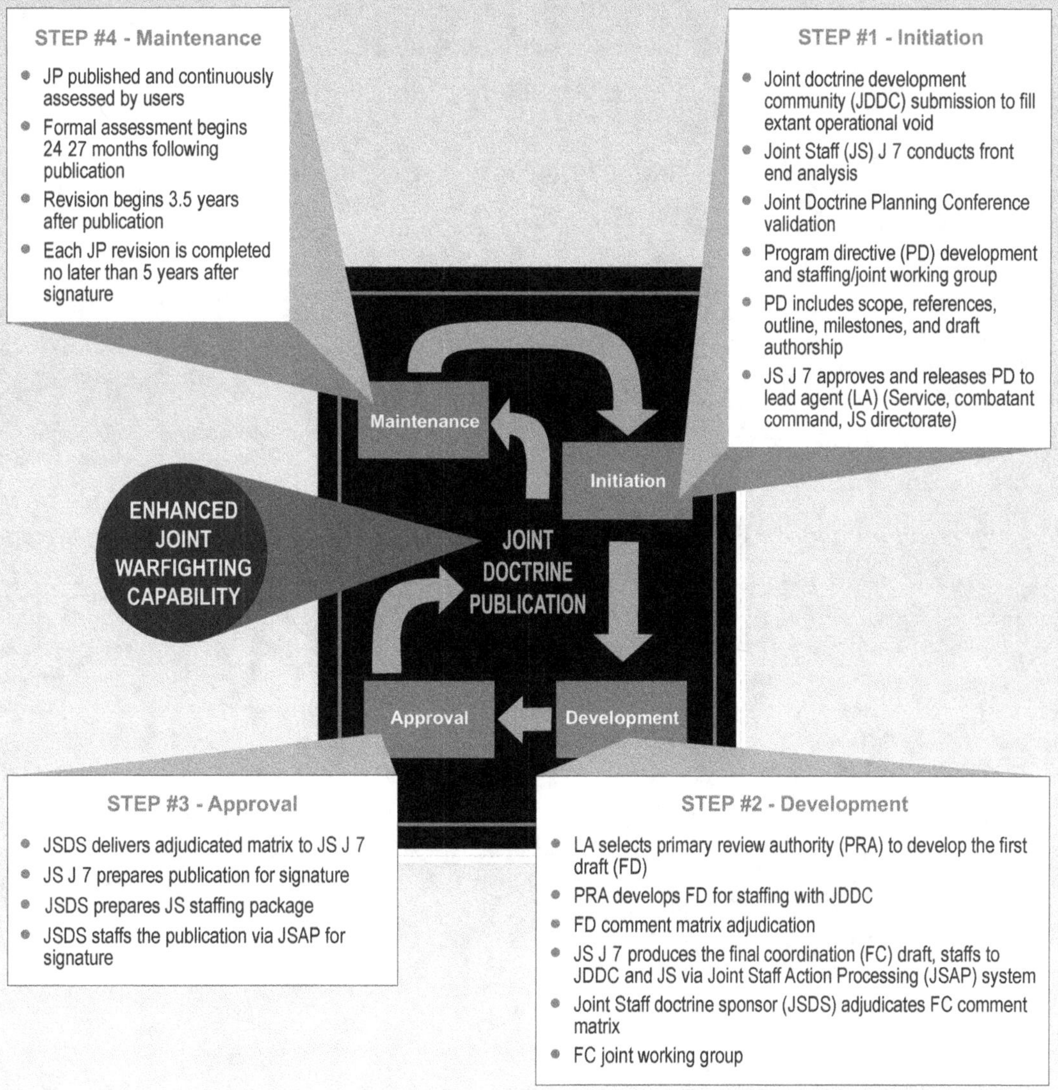

STEP #4 - Maintenance
JP published and continuously assessed by users
Formal assessment begins 24 27 months following publication
Revision begins 3.5 years after publication
Each JP revision is completed no later than 5 years after signature
STEP #1 - Initiation
Joint doctrine development community (JDDC) submission to fill extant operational void
Joint Staff (JS) J 7 conducts front end analysis
Joint Doctrine Planning Conference validation
Program directive (PD) development and staffing/joint working group
PD includes scope, references, outline, milestones, and draft authorship
JS J 7 approves and releases PD to lead agent (LA) (Service, combatant command, JS directorate)
Maintenance
Initiation
ENHANCED JOINT WARFIGHTING CAPABILITY
JOINT DOCTRINE PUBLICATION
Approval
Development
STEP #3 - Approval
JSDS delivers adjudicated matrix to JS J 7
JS J 7 prepares publication for signature
JSDS prepares JS staffing package
JSDS staffs the publication via JSAP for signature
STEP #2 - Development
LA selects primary review authority (PRA) to develop the first draft (FD)
PRA develops FD for staffing with JDDC
FD comment matrix adjudication
JS J 7 produces the final coordination (FC) draft, staffs to JDDC and JS via Joint Staff Action Processing (JSAP) system
Joint Staff doctrine sponsor (JSDS) adjudicates FC comment matrix
FC joint working group